Riding for pleasure

An easy-going
practical guide

to

Heike Lebherz

Riding for pleasure

An easy-going
practical guide
to learning
to ride for fun

D&C
David and Charles

A DAVID & CHARLES BOOK
David & Charles is a subsidiary of F+W (UK) Ltd.,
an F+W Publications Inc. company

First published in the UK in 2005

Copyright © 2003 BLV Verlagsgesellschaft mbH, München/GERMANY
Title of the original German edition: JUST FUN – Reitkurs für Erwachsene

Distributed in North America
by F+W Publications, Inc.
4700 East Galbraith Road
Cincinnati, OH 45236
1-800-289-0963

A catalogue record for this book is available from the British Library.

ISBN 0 7153 2097 1

Horse care and riding is not without risk, and while the authors and
publishers have made every attempt to offer accurate and reliable
information to the best of their knowledge and belief, it is presented without
any guarantee. The authors and publishers therefore disclaim any liability
incurred in connection with using the information contained in this book.

Printed in Singapore by KHL Printing Co. Pte Ltd
for David & Charles
Brunel House   Newton Abbot   Devon

Visit our website at www.davidandcharles.co.uk

David & Charles books are available from all good bookshops; alternatively
you can contact our Orderline on (0)1626 334555 or write to us at FREEPOST
EX2 110, David & Charles Direct, Newton Abbot, TQ12 4ZZ (no stamp
required UK mainland).

Contents

Tuning up

Foreword

Dear reader,

This book is a result of the experiences, thoughts and feelings that I have had over more than 30 years spent with horses, and many years of working with novice riders. Through it, I hope to instil you with enthusiasm for a hobby that has no equal. I am sure that once you have been introduced to the most glorious creature in the world, you will be a rider for life.

It is an undeniable fact that people who have been around horses and learnt how to ride as children do have an advantage. Much that falls effortlessly into a child's lap needs to be worked for hard as an adult. But this hard work is well worthwhile, because it is possible to ride well into old age. Sadly, many adult beginner riders despair early on in their riding careers and a good number give up before they have got anywhere. I hope this book will go a good way towards preventing this. It might even contribute to some riding schools reconsidering their teaching methods for adult learners. The book aims to show you what you need to learn, what you must remember and how you should go about attaining the goals you set yourself. Think of it as a kind of preparation for your entire riding life, whether you simply want to ride once a week at a riding school, or to become more heavily involved in riding, setting yourself and your horse many different challenges. Whatever your ambitions, you need a solid and comprehensive foundation for your own good and, of course, for that of your horse. Having a solid foundation is really the only way to enjoy your riding and to be safe and confident. Even if your primary reason for wanting to start riding is for the exercise, it is important not to undervalue this basic knowledge. In addition, the skills you will learn from reading this book will put you well ahead of many of your fellow learner riders.

In the following pages you will also find out a great deal about horses themselves – what makes them tick. It is vital to remember that riding is a team sport and the team is a partnership of human and horse. As rider, you bear the responsibility for your partner and the only way you can be a good partner is to fully understand and be considerate towards your other half.

Finally, I'd like to conjure up a glint in your eyes, and those of your horse, a glint I would like to see much more often when I watch people ride. I'd like to wish you an enjoyable read, and an enjoyable start to your riding experiences!

Wanting
to learn
to ride,
and what you need to know

Nowadays, more and more people are looking for a way to live a life that is closer to nature. As part of this enthusiasm for a more natural life, it makes sense that there is also an ever-increasing interest in horses. Frequently, it isn't only children who are standing, eyes shining, by the paddock fence, but many adults too.

Things to remember at the
start

You must dare
to leave the paths you know
so that new horizons
can open up for you.

In riding, you have chosen a hobby without equal. Your partner isn't a friend you play tennis with every so often, but a creature that is very different from you in many ways. A horse.

....

One of the great joys of riding is being able to take a leisurely walk through the countryside (below) ... or let your horse paddle in a cool stream (right).

....

Unfortunately for horses, they are not in a position to choose their partner. When someone decides to hop up on their back, they have no choice in the matter. Don't forget that horses live in a state of total dependence on humans. They are entrusted to our care and are

Tip

+ Unfortunately, some riding schools persist in treating adult beginners as peripheral curiosities. However, there are good schools out there where you will be taught with care and respect. Choose one of these. If you are not happy with your school, change to another one.

completely at our mercy. If you are fully aware of this, and use your position of power only for the protection and wellbeing of the horse, you will make a lifelong friend of your horse.

As you think about how much you'd like to ride, you probably imagine idyllic rides into the countryside, choreographed dressage sessions on a powerful but gentle horse, leaping ditches or fences, or enjoying tranquil moments as your equine partner plucks at wisps of grass. All your dreams can come true, as long as you do not expect everything at once.

Which of the following two phrases best describes you? Be honest. I expect the maximum possible result for the minimum effort in the shortest possible time. I am prepared to assess my own actions and abilities honestly and fairly, and to commit myself to a decent portion of self-discipline. If you tend towards the first phrase, don't even bother to start riding. If you set ambitious goals for yourself in riding, you must also be

prepared to invest time and patience in achieving them. There will be a lot in this learning process that doesn't work perfectly to begin with. But that doesn't matter, because you are on the right course if you're starting to think along these lines.

The usual picture

Some of you might recognize some of the situations I'm about to describe. If you're an adult learner, it's probably precisely because of these or similar that you abandoned your riding dreams long ago, before you had the chance to start making them into reality. It isn't too late. Just start again, and start in the way I describe here. As you read this book, I hope that you will find it outlines riding the way you hoped it would be – maybe your riding school did things differently. Change your perspective. Go and find a school that can offer you this kind of basic work, and start to acquire what you have missed up to now in your riding training.

Sadly, there are still a great many riding schools using 'tried and trusted' methods, obviously having failed to notice that, in the world outside, treatment of horses and riding students has been updated. Adult learners particularly are rarely taken seriously in such schools. Often the beginners' classes peter out into a few dreary and meaningless sessions on the lunge. As soon as the student is halfway capable of being on a horse, he or she is shunted off into a group lesson due to pressure of time or lack of organization. With luck, some friendly stable girl might show you how to groom or saddle a horse. But in this kind of riding school, too many

questions are not welcomed. If you do ask about something, the answer will probably be, 'Because that's the way it is!'

It is unlikely that you will ever really enjoy yourself when you go to this sort of riding school. No one here will help you get over the feeling that you are completely out of your depth in this alien new world. Your anxiety at the unaccustomed contact with the horse, your fear of falling off and any insecurity arising from what you know you don't know will also be unchallenged. Once your riding instructor has thoroughly run you down, you'll probably end up asking yourself: What am I doing here? Do I really have to do this?

Was your riding school like this? Did you experience an unpleasant sinking feeling in the pit of your stomach before each lesson? Or maybe you recognize the feeling of being grateful that an unavoidable appointment

Maybe I should saddle up my bike instead?

Angi Johnson's first group riding lesson

Angela Johnson, Angi to her friends, is 38 years old and loves horses. A while ago, she decided to make her childhood dream come true, and finally learn to ride.

No sooner said than done. I won't describe the first four lunge sessions here; it isn't worth the effort. But then, Mary, assistant instructor and responsible for *all* lunge sessions, falls victim to – no, not chronic dizziness – the flu. Things are about to get exciting. As Angi enters the tackroom on the afternoon of her lesson, Jim Laurel, the head riding instructor – late fifties, neat and trim, small Clark Gable moustache – applies the smile that is the speciality of his profession. 'Well, Mrs Johnson, at long last a ray of sunshine on this gloomy day.' (If only he hadn't had a few beers at lunchtime, his vision might be clearer, too.) 'Today you will take part in your first group riding lesson. Don't be nervous, you have a natural talent, you'll be fine.'

A few minutes later, eyes shining, knees shaking, Angi stands outside Trigger's stable. 'Oh, what a good horse you are,' she breathes respectfully and nervously. Trigger isn't really all that impressed. Ears pinned back, he turns his powerful hindquarters in her direction and makes no special effort to take part in this exchange. And now, thrown in at the deep end, Angi is alone with Trigger, a saddle and a bridle, bound for the wide green world. All too soon a voice bawls in the distance, 'Hurry up, lesson starts in ten minutes!' Pandemonium breaks out in the neighbouring stables.

'No worries, Trigger, we're going to be fine, aren't we?' says Angi, her voice already cracking, as she opens the stable door. After several minutes of anguish and tears, Angi finally succeeds in getting this monster on four legs saddled and tacked up. (I won't go into more details here about which straps are in the wrong place, which ones are not fastened at all and which are sort of lashed together any old how.)

Dragging Trigger along behind her, she makes her way into the riding arena. It's already bustling with activity, and Jim Laurel gives her an encouraging smile. Somehow she manages to clamber on board the horse, and then she finds fate taking its course. The charming riding instructor is transformed from Dr Jekyll to Mr Hyde, becoming a raging beast.

Several times Angi hears the words, 'Pull yourself together, for crying out loud, you're sitting there like a sack of flour on a workhorse! Back straight, heels doooooooown!!!'

Trigger, who has finally had enough (of the noise, the sack of flour and just generally everything), breaks into a canter. Angela Johnson parts company with his back (with a triple salchow of Olympic dexterity that would astonish the ice-skating world), with one of her carefully polished fingernails, and, last and least, with the riding school. The resemblance between the expression on her face and that on Trigger's is remarkable.

A pity.

made you have to cancel the next one, and the next. And one day you just didn't go back. But here you are again, by the paddock fence or in the spectators' stand, looking longingly at these wonderful creatures that you'd love to spend time with and learn to ride. Go on, seize the moment! Find a riding school that can help you fulfil your dream. There are methods of teaching you to ride and be with horses that are based on enjoyment rather than frustration. It's worth travelling further to find such a school. Because, in the end, it is your hobby, and the idea is to have fun.

Riding is good for your mind!

It is said that the person must be dominant in the horse-human partnership. But 'dominant' in this case is too often misinterpreted.

Spending time with a horse can bring huge amounts of enjoyment into your life.

So instead of talking about dominance, let's talk about guiding excellence. Of these two personality types that you might recognize from your everyday life, which one is more likely to be taken seriously as a leader: the bigmouth who seizes every opportunity to stamp about, yelling, and at whose appearance all conversation dries up? The one who snaps, 'That's what I pay you for!' whenever you have a problem, but won't make the slightest effort to tackle difficulties himself? The one who puts you under enormous psychological pressure, making you feel useless at everything you do? Or the one whose calm character, excellent powers of persuasion, professional competence and friendly aura motivate you, so that you would go through fire for him? The one who lets you get more than just a word in edgeways at brainstorming sessions, and who is always prepared to listen to your ideas?

Now, you're probably asking, 'What does brainstorming have to do with horses? What ideas is my riding-school horse going to be offering to me?' Well, just you wait and see. You will get surprising answers to both of those questions in your riding life.

In communication with your horse, you'll notice how important it is to set aside certain negative character traits, and to focus your mind more strongly on your better self. The traits you must never indulge are rage, outbursts of temper, impatience, egotism and weakness. For lasting enjoyment with horses and riding – and, of course, any parallels with the rest of life are purely coincidental – you'll need patience, fairness, self-discipline, self-awareness, consistency, friendliness, respect and humility.

As you'll find out in more detail later, in 'The mind of the horse' (see page 34), the horse is a herd animal. Since every herd is governed by a defined hierarchy, the question of 'who's the boss?' also arises in the

A proven
concept

+ Therapeutic riding is widely used as a form of treatment for certain illnesses and disabilities, and thanks to the unique characteristics of the horse it has achieved demonstrable success.

+ At the same time, it has been shown that these techniques do not only provide benefits in the field of therapy. Their benefits are felt among all people who want to learn to ride and experience riding in a different way that takes into account their individual and personal attributes. Children, young people and adults – especially those returning to riding or beginning to fulfil their childhood dreams – all feel that they gain more than simply a physical skill when they ride.

+ Holistic techniques enable people to understand horses as living beings, and to become friends with them. They learn everything connected with caring for and grooming the animals. Because at first the rider does nothing but pay attention to the movement of the horse and his own sensations, the early riding experience is without any kind of performance anxiety, and so without fear. *All* the senses are addressed, and needs and emotions are awakened, to be fulfilled by the horse.

Gabi Schreiber (educator, qualified riding instructor, Swiss Therapeutic Riding Association)

In spite of all obstacles

+ As a 15-year-old, I had the chance to ride while on a school trip in the country.

+ The relaxed atmosphere and wonderful countryside made it great fun. But when I got home and started going to a riding school, I soon realized it wasn't for me. The horses were unhappy, the costs were extortionate and the atmosphere at the school dreadful.

+ After a gap of many years my 22-year-old daughter persuaded me to take a part-time job in a local riding school, mucking out stables. My friends laughed and asked me if I was going to become a groom. But for me, it was a wonderful opportunity to make a connection, quietly, with the horses. I enjoyed it so much that I applied for the next adult learning course. I'm not afraid, because my knowledge of the horses enables me to go about everything quite calmly. My daughter is also taking lessons, and we're dreaming of riding out together for the first time very soon.

Joy – 53

relationship between human and horse. Don't shrug this off as irrelevant just because you're only going to be having a little trot around the arena once a week. Ten seconds on a horse can become an eternity if he decides to take matters into his own hands! This fact shouldn't fill you with fear, but instead thoroughly convince you that it is essential to clarify your status – unambiguously.

A horse's relationship with you is based on trust and the feeling of being protected; only when he has these will he accept you as boss. This requires a high level of self-discipline in you, because a brief excursion into the territory of the loudmouth can quickly destroy much of your hard-won trust. Riding, if you learn it in its entirety, has a wonderfully relaxing effect, and is unparalleled as a leisure activity – you won't believe how good it is for your mind to get up at the crack of dawn on a Sunday morning to go out on your horse and exercise your soul. Before you start your actual riding lessons, think about what you expect from the partnership between you and your horse. Never lose sight of the welfare of the horse while considering this. In reality, when all is said and done, what you want to learn is not a sporting technique, but how to communicate with another living being.

Don't be put off by the thought of this. It is hard work, but what you receive in return, if you're prepared to tackle everything to do with riding and understanding horses, is so utterly wonderful that it's worth every effort. If you've mastered the basic concepts of riding, can control your horse reliably and have clearly established your 'dominant' status, you'll feel marvellous, because it is a real pleasure to be at one with this remarkable animal.

Anyone can attain this goal, but the road there is a long one. You need to be prepared for a bit of a slog, and have a burning interest in constantly learning more about horses and a decent portion of staying power and patience. Learning to ride and to work with horses is, however, tremendous fun, in spite of the muscular aches and pains you'll get to start with – which you can, in any case, minimize with warm-up exercises (see page 28).

Info

+ To ride you need physical fitness, a good sense of balance and sharp reactions, but also patience, a sense of justice, self-discipline and humility. You can train up the physical side, but you'll need to bring the mental attitude with you.

Riding will change you, and for the better. Just thinking consciously about the character traits lurking in all of us is a good start. Consciously preventing negative reactions, or not allowing them to arise in the first place, doesn't only improve your relationship with horses, it'll also get you more friends in everyday life. And if working on a bit of self-discipline makes you a little friendlier towards all the creatures of the earth, learning to ride will have been even more worthwhile. Part of the fascination that horses exert on people comes from the fact that we can learn so much from them. One thing is beyond doubt: riding is good for your mind!

Spending time on such a lovely hobby is enough to put anyone into a good mood.

No dough, no show

You've discovered a wonderful hobby. You want it to bring you pleasure, not frustration, and you certainly don't want any harm to come of it.

In that case, it's worth spending money. For good, professional services, for decent equipment – to do the thing properly.

Whatever you do, don't decide which riding school to attend on the basis of your wallet. Of course, we all have a certain threshold of financial pain, a comfort zone for what we're prepared to spend on a hobby, and 'money is no object' is something only a lucky few can honestly say. But I urge you, now at the start of your riding career and from then on, not to scrimp and save in the wrong places. Excellence is expensive and can only be provided if the business offering it is able to make enough money to budget for it – your day-to-day life should have taught you that.

If you choose the right riding school, in return for your cash, you can expect to be taught on calm, well-trained, healthy horses by a sympathetic experienced teacher and this will make your first riding lessons a true pleasure – again, despite those inevitable aches and pains. Remember as well that the horses you ride have to be fed and cared for all year round – even when you perhaps don't go riding so often, when you're on holiday or ill, or when the weather's bad. Such a service has its costs.

So please bear all this in mind when the time comes to lay a couple more banknotes on the table. Be honest, didn't you come to this hobby because you love horses? Well, don't be stingy when you're lucky enough to find a good riding school nearby, and it feels exactly right.

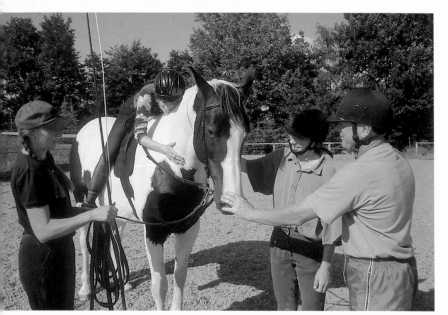

Left: Thank you, it's been such fun for all of us.
Right top: Horses love this sort of living.
Right bottom: In the right hands, your first ride out will be great fun.

Check-list

Riding schools

A good riding school **CANNOT** offer these things at bargain basement prices:

○ Appropriate treatment of horses with airy, bright stables and suitable paddocks.

○ Fenced-in grazing all year round.

○ A good choice of school horses, all of which get some time off.

○ Impeccable veterinary care including dental checks, worming and inoculation.

○ Suitable and well-maintained saddlery.

○ Regular hoof checks and good shoeing.

○ Well-trained, professional staff, who are friendly, competent and patient, who work individually with you and the animals and also take the time to train themselves.

○ Riding lessons that are not a mass demonstration, but happen in small groups and with a positive atmosphere.

○ A peaceful retirement for horses that have finished active riding-school work.

The time factor

It's fundamentally true that riding is a time-consuming hobby. Don't let that discourage you, though, because with good time management, you'll still be able to find space for it in your life.

At the start, you should certainly invest plenty of time, because the more intensively you can tackle this new world, the sooner you'll be at home in it. Read as much as you can about horses, and seek them out whenever and wherever you can, in order to study them and their unique behaviour. Timewise, learning to ride has aspects that are short-, medium- and long-term.

In the beginning was the aching muscle

One of the *short-term aspects* of learning to ride is muscular aches and pains, and the only thing to do with these is to see them through. Try to take riding lessons at least once or twice a week, and do some other keep-fit activities too. You'll soon notice how good it is for you if you stick at it. And don't just train your body – work too to improve your perceptions and reflexes, and to develop your understanding of everything to do with horses. This means spending a lot of time at the stable, not just being there when you have a riding lesson. Listen, watch, observe the horses, help with the stable chores if possible – everything that's going on will teach you a great deal.

Left: Even collecting horse manure can broaden your horizons.
Right: There is something for everyone on this walk.

Persistence is the motto

In the *medium term*, you need to have fixed riding dates each week.

It's essential to have regular riding lessons, without too long an interval in between. Most practical of all is to go on short, intensive courses alongside your weekly riding lessons. These courses are often held at weekends and they can teach you a great deal in a compressed form. There are so many courses on a wide variety of subjects, that you'll find it difficult to choose between them. Among the most useful are courses in groundwork, equine anatomy and psychology, as well as all-round safety and confidence building. It's also worth getting hold of horsey textbooks and reading them carefully in peace and quiet to deepen your theoretical knowledge. From a technical point of view, however, it's sensible to have one instructor at the beginning of your riding life. Otherwise it can be confusing, because every teacher will have their own pet methods, and will explain particular techniques in different ways.

Dreaming on

You still have some time to think about the *long term*. By then, perhaps the question of getting your own horse will come up. An alternative is to consider borrowing or sharing someone else's horse. All of these involve tremendous responsibility, with all that entails. Before you take a horse on, please consider the implications very carefully. Your own horse is like a member of the family. You can't just leave it in the garage for a week or two because you're a bit busy. It's a living creature, not a piece of sporting equipment. In addition, you have to be fair to your horse, no matter how you feel. The rule is this: with horses, you must

learn how to flick a 'calmness switch' inside yourself when you are around them, even if your day has been full of stress. It is only through calmness and patience that you will get the results that you are hoping for and working towards – to be able to enjoy riding and caring for your horse, both of you feeling relaxed and happy and at one with each other.

You can't learn to ride overnight. There is an infinite amount involved in the business of learning about a creature, like the horse, that is so different from us. It's the work of many years to understand all its complexities and, in fact, you'll never stop learning. Even when you have become a good rider, you will still have startling moments of insight. But that's just what makes riding so interesting, because teamwork with a horse is a mental game, bringing lifelong enjoyment and constantly presenting you with new challenges. So keep at it, and take pleasure in the slightest progress. If you accept these tiny forward steps – and also the many lulls – success will come all the sooner.

It's worth all your efforts, and all the time you invest.

On not spoiling things for
choice (of a riding school)

I've said it before, but it is worth repeating: take enormous care in choosing a riding school, because in the end it's the foundation riding work that determines your future course as a rider.

Whatever you miss or mistake in the early stages will get in your way further down the road. Techniques wrongly learned have a habit of rooting themselves stubbornly in your mind and are extremely difficult to correct. Whatever you aim to do in the end – jumping, dressage or simply riding for pleasure – the basic skills are the same. Therefore, you need to learn these

Tip

+ As a beginner, whether your want to trot across country on a sure-footed cob, ride Western-style on a spotted Appaloosa or practise 'haute école' on a noble Warmblood, it doesn't matter. Because, different as the riding styles and training methods are, they all have the same basic underlying aim, which is to create a perfect partnership between the horse and rider, a team working in harmony with minimal communication. In addition, all teaching concentrates on rider skills, such as balance, so the horse doesn't suffer any discomfort.

Above: Close collaboration between student and instructor in the early stages is vital.
Right: Capturing the heart via the stomach.

fundamentals. The combination of understanding the horse, acquiring knowledge of everything concerning horses, and learning the practicalities on the ground and in the saddle, will set you on course to attain the goal you long for. If you forget any one of these three points, the result will always be unsatisfactory, and the one to suffer most when things go wrong is the horse. A good riding school will not only teach you riding technique, but will also familiarize you with the horse.

Sniff around – thoroughly

Take a quiet look around the riding school during the working day. How are the lessons organized? Is there intensive work in small groups? How does the instructor react to students? Does he just trail through the riding lesson looking bored, or does he take an active interest in solving problems? Do beginners and more advanced students ride around among one another, or is it clear that riders are working in defined groups? Pay attention to the range of choices available in riding courses and lessons. Are there trial lessons to offer a taster? Specialized courses, in groundwork perhaps, or theory sessions?

Happy horses with space and freedom

Look at the horses, watch how they are treated. Are they all, including the learners' horses, given access to enough exercise space, and are they in roomy stables? Of course, horses are ridden out, but they need much more freedom and exercise than they get from a couple of riding lessons to satisfy their needs and keep them healthy.

Imagine this: you stand, day in, day out, for about 23 hours a day in a tiny room hardly big enough to walk around without bumping into something. You have no contact with other people. And your senses get no stimulation. The only diversions, if you're lucky, are three meals a day. But even they are meagre and eaten

up in no time, because you're not supposed to get fat. You know that your stomach and digestive system are suffering. Your legs and back are becoming stiff and sore from too much standing around, and you now fear

A nice
place to be
a horse

An ideal way of housing a horse is in a well-lit airy stable with free access to an enclosed exercise area, so that he can decide for himself where to spend his time. This will prevent boredom and allow a certain amount of activity when he needs it. Some additional social contact over the fence will increase the level of activity and keep the horse in good physical shape for exercise. The fresh air, free of dust and relatively unpolluted by harmful ammonia gas, is also extremely healthy. On the other hand, when the horses want to rest, they can. Controlled, individual feeding and care are also possible.

A room complete with a view and a fly curtain.

the moment when someone comes to fetch you out of your room, because they will force you straight into a session of exercise without warming up first. You're also out of condition because of lack of exercise, and the bad air in the room irritates your sensitive respiratory passages. Day by day you are becoming more miserable, and at some point you will give up altogether. Sadly, even today, the daily stable life of many horses is like this. Of course, no one can just release a yard full of horses into a paddock and leave them to their own devices. That would be the opposite extreme, and it simply isn't practicable. An alternative with much to recommend it, though, is the 'room with balcony, including daily group fitness training', in other words, a loose box or stall with a daily group run out in the paddock.

Providing horses with time out together in a paddock or corral gives them the chance to feel free, at least for a while. They can let off steam, exercise their hierarchical behaviour, fulfil their need to play, groom their coats, have a good roll around if they feel like it, and generally be themselves. In other words, be horses! Of course, this kind of arrangement requires a great deal of planning and investment at the start. But it does repay everything because it makes the horses healthier and improves their performance. It makes more sense to pay for some fencing for an extra paddock rather than use the money on sky-high vet's bills.

For you as a beginner, a contented horse that is happy to work with you, with plenty of scope to satisfy its instincts when you aren't sitting on it, is also much safer. So pay attention to how the horse is kept, even if it doesn't belong to you. By going to a good riding school rather than a poor one, you will be supporting the proper treatment of horses.

Trust your instincts

Before making a final decision about a riding school think things through carefully. Was the atmosphere right? Would you feel good there? It is important for you to feel happy in the place where you learn to ride. Only then will you want to be there outside lesson times, always coming back with a good, relaxed feeling. It isn't only when choosing a dentist or financial advisor that the chemistry needs to be right: it applies to choosing a riding instructor too.

Beware also of so-called, often self-appointed gurus, of whom there are plenty. Real horsemen and women will never praise their own method above all others as the one true holy one. Of course, they trust a particular method of teaching because it has proved itself to them through many years of experience. However, good instructors are always prepared to think about other riding styles and to incorporate some aspects of them in their own work.

Once you have provisionally chosen a riding school, visit it quietly once or twice more. Every business can have a day that is better or worse than normal. If your feeling is that things could go well here, then it's time to give it a try. You will quickly find out whether or not the decision was right. Even the best riding school cannot entirely spare you from aches and pains, but it can spare you frustration. So, if you feel frustrated, start searching again – because learning to ride is supposed to be fun!

It's such a pleasure to be able to scratch yourself when it itches.

Tough question:
what shall I wear?

You might have to compromise on the question of clothing. And you may not be able to wear the latest fashions. Accept this before going to get your kit.

Safety is the first commandment so your riding hat must conform to current industry standards. Modern technology has led to the production of ultra-light hats and helmets, some with ventilation holes, that will not do too much damage to the hairstyle contained within. Crash helmets save lives, and not only when people fall off their horse. If you are riding out along a beautiful, blossoming avenue of trees, and inadvertently knock your head on a branch, your dearest wish will be to be wearing a good helmet.

Footloose, not footsore

Footwear must be strong, ankle- or knee-high and not too broad across the balls of the feet, so that the boot does not stick in the stirrup. Just occasionally, horses have been known to plant their whole weight on a human foot via a single hoof, so it's a good idea to make sure you wear strong boots. Quality long leather riding boots cost a small fortune and, particularly early

Left: Get ahead, get a hat.
Above: Watch out for branches!

on, they aren't necessary. There are plenty of reasonably priced ankle boots available, in which you can quite happily, and above all comfortably, put quite a distance behind you on foot if you have to. If you choose ankle boots, it's a good idea to wear half chaps – a flexible boot leg-piece with a zip or other closure on the side. These are effective at preventing chafing on the legs as the stirrup strap rubs against them.

What about underwear?

Underwear is also well worth thinking about. Even if your personal taste veers in the direction of a string tanga, you're much better off in something more conventional. You will be grateful for this advice! Even lace will have your bottom begging for mercy after an hour's ride. Good, functional sports underwear is the most appropriate choice for all physical exercise.

Other kit

When trying on riding trousers, the more mature riders among us will find that 'size 12' (or a 34-inch waist, depending on your gender) is not what it once was. Unfortunately, it makes little sense to appear before your horse dressed to the nines, and to get no further than eye contact because your legs are so tightly encased that you can't mount. Close-fitting jodhpurs made from elasticated materials are highly recommended. They are practical and comfortable and are ideal for wearing over ankle boots. For lessons, don't wear tops that are too baggy or big, otherwise your riding instructor will not be able to tell if you are sitting straight. You should also dress in layers, like an onion. Why? Well, while grooming the horse, grappling with saddlery, working in the stable, exercising with the

Tips

+ Don't buy trousers that are too tight – choose one size bigger (you don't need to tell anyone). For groundwork and exercises, jogging pants or jeans are fine.

+ Wear clothes suited to the situation. If you will actually be riding, wear proper riding breeches or jodphurs. Jeans can cause painful chafing, and jogging pants will soon have you sliding off. Breeches or jodphurs give you a good contact with the saddle. Modern fibres are easy to care for and are hard-wearing.

+ Many equestrian shops have a bargain corner where seasonal articles are taken out of the regular range and sold off at cut prices.

horse and so on, you can become quite warm. Then you can take off your jacket and sweater and work on in your T-shirt. As soon as your body is at rest, it's a good idea at least to put the sweater back on, because there is always a draught somewhere, even in indoor schools. You need to be equipped for all these changes. Above all, make sure your riding clothes are comfortable. Staff at any specialist equestrian equipment shop will gladly advise you about suitable clothing. For the moment, there's no need to give any thought to crops, spurs or other accessories.

Unless your riding school dictates otherwise, wear casual clothing. The horse is not going to be swayed by your appearance. It might be swayed by the carrots you have hidden in the capacious pockets of your jacket.

No pain, no gain?

Into the saddle and off you go?
Not quite.

Depending on age, physique and fitness, every beginner rider should consider what physical exercises should accompany their new hobby. Over time, many adults have become slightly, or even entirely, physically rusty. That doesn't matter, because you're going to start slowly. Of course, every sporting activity involves a certain risk of injury, but training to build up physical strength can minimize this risk. And if you can sometimes exercise on and with the horse, you will hardly see it as an unpleasant chore to be done as quickly as possible.

Build the following activities into your weekly timetable (also, start every day with some stretching under the bedcovers):

Fitness for two

✛ Training the horse trains the rider too: both are required to do symmetrical work, which helps to balance out our natural left- or right-handedness.

✛ Demands are also placed on postural mechanisms (such as the musculature of the abdomen and back) to produce a stabilizing effect; today these mechanisms are the most poorly exercised of all.

Eva Rehm (physiotherapist)

– *Jogging* or *Walking* to build up condition. Once or twice a week, jog or walk for half an hour in the fresh air. This will do you good. You'll learn to breathe consciously and evenly, and an even breathing rhythm will help you with both endurance training and riding.
– *Swimming* trains your whole body.
– *Gym work* – for example, stomach-leg-buttock work – is useful for more precise development of individual muscle groups. You can get more ideas from books.

No pain, no gain!

– But now for the pièce de résistance! *Lambada dancing* – it loosens up the swing of your hips, and that is indispensable in riding. Once you're on horseback, you'll understand why. If you prefer, you can also reach for a hula hoop.

To activate your sense of balance and your reactions, you just need to persuade yourself to rediscover all those childhood joys. Balance on logs. From now on, only run on the white line separating the pavement from the cycle path. Hop on one leg, stand on one leg at the baker's or the butcher's! Put together your own individual training programme. This will also challenge your mind. You'll be amazed at how much fun it is to become more active again. Get yourself off the sofa. Turn somersaults again. A skilful, well-landed somersault has made many a fall from a horse quite harmless.

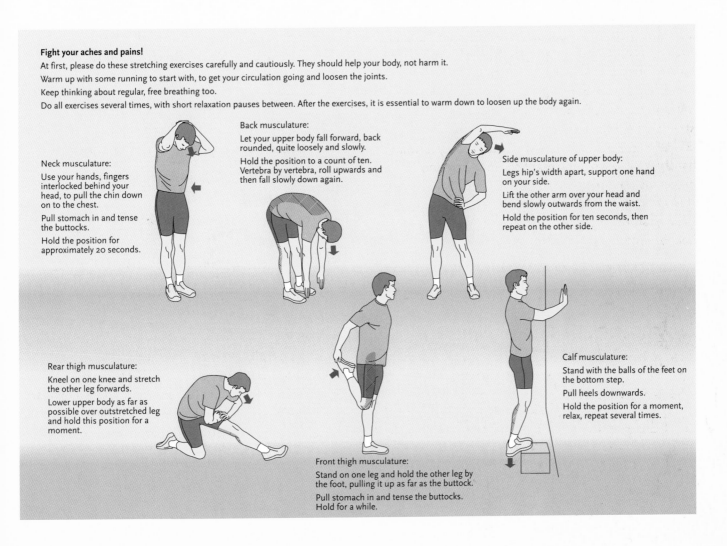

Fight your aches and pains!
At first, please do these stretching exercises carefully and cautiously. They should help your body, not harm it.
Warm up with some running to start with, to get your circulation going and loosen the joints.
Keep thinking about regular, free breathing too.
Do all exercises several times, with short relaxation pauses between. After the exercises, it is essential to warm down to loosen up the body again.

Neck musculature:

Use your hands, fingers interlocked behind your head, to pull the chin down on to the chest.

Pull stomach in and tense the buttocks.

Hold the position for approximately 20 seconds.

Back musculature:

Let your upper body fall forward, back rounded, quite loosely and slowly.

Hold the position to a count of ten. Vertebra by vertebra, roll upwards and then fall slowly down again.

Side musculature of upper body:

Legs hip's width apart, support one hand on your side.

Lift the other arm over your head and bend slowly outwards from the waist.

Hold the position for ten seconds, then repeat on the other side.

Rear thigh musculature:

Kneel on one knee and stretch the other leg forwards.

Lower upper body as far as possible over outstretched leg and hold this position for a moment.

Front thigh musculature:

Stand on one leg and hold the other leg by the foot, pulling it up as far as the buttock.

Pull stomach in and tense the buttocks. Hold for a while.

Calf musculature:

Stand with the balls of the feet on the bottom step.

Pull heels downwards.

Hold the position for a moment, relax, repeat several times.

What you need to know about horses

All the happiness on earth is found on the back of a horse... However hackneyed this saying might seem, there is plenty of truth in it. Learning to ride, to create a harmonious partnership with a horse — these experiences are unbeatable. It is a wonderful heart-warming feeling to gain the trust of this animal that is so superior to us in strength and has so little need of our friendship.

Thoughts about your **partner** – the horse

We all know from our daily lives that we must be there for friends when they need us.

In our relationships with horses, this means to treat them in a way that is as appropriate to their nature as possible, and to behave in the same way when we spend time with them. Give the horse a space in which he feels good. This applies as much to how he is kept as to his position within the human-horse hierarchy. Don't just learn to ride – learn *everything* about horses' needs. These wonderful animals are such a joy to us, and we also owe them a debt.

Tip

+ Every novice rider should start by trying to sense the quality of movement in the partner beneath him in all paces, because the main cause of disturbance in the horse's movement apparatus is the rider.

Kalle Rehm (equine osteopath and physiotherapist)

Comprehensive horse sense can only be built up through a broad basic training, supported by good textbooks and careful observation. You should also always keep this book in your hands, because that means that you will be thinking, and thinking alone is a giant step along the way to that worthwhile goal: an ideal partnership with the horse.

The ideal: the all-doing genetically engineered animal

Do you dream of a speckled Appaloosa or a noble Andalusian? Both excellent wishes. Once you have really

It is no fun being thirsty, even if you are otherwise well looked after.

learned to ride, you can fulfil these wishes and buy your own horse. But during your learning phase, you should entrust yourself to horses that are suited to the job of training you. Above all, it is important to match horse and rider sizewise. For example, ponies are not suitable for an adult, unless you are a tiny adult, mainly because of your weight, but also because you will find it difficult to achieve the correct leg position if two thirds of your leg are hanging out below the pony's stomach. Ponies are great for children, however. If you are quite short, you will be assailed by a fear of heights if someone perches you on top of an 18-hand giant. Many adult beginners therefore prefer medium-sized horses, which are manageable in the truest sense of the word. Naturally, a school horse should be basically healthy. Who could be happy knowing that a sick horse was suffering beneath them?

In terms of temperament, a calm animal, not disposed to panic, but still with a cheerful forward impetus about it, is ideal. Its character and nature should be impeccable, and its tolerance of rider errors rather high. A good basic training will soon ensure that you as a student will be able to feel for yourself when you have done something wrong.

The horse should, of course, also have an aptitude for dressage, jumping and cross-country. In fact, what we are looking for is a real all-round talent, or, to put it another way, an all-doing genetically engineered animal. Are you, as a riding student, prepared to foot the bill? You must reckon on a certain amount of expenditure if the horses you are going to learn on are to carry out their demanding job. Be aware from the outset that this creature bringing so much pleasure to your life is itself a living being with its own – costly – needs.

How much can a horse's
back carry?

+ The carrying capacity of a horse's back depends on its musculature, which is improved via suitable exercises while it is being trained and training you. The sitting ability of the rider also influences the horse's load tolerance: an unco-ordinated beginner weighing 60kg (132lb) is heavier for the horse to carry than a good rider who weighs 80kg (176lb) but who is in harmony with the horse's movements.

A well-muscled horse's back can easily carry two adults for short spells.

The mind of the horse

The horse is a herd animal and a flight animal. You need to bear this in mind when you interact with it.

If you want to get to know a horse's mind well, you must observe horses intensively, and read a few books on the subject too.

Scratch my back, and I'll scratch yours

Thousands of years ago, the horse lived wild on the steppes in free hunting-grounds, and horses still have the instincts and reflexes from that time today. They live in a herd, which offers them protection and safety. Within the group there is a strict hierarchy, and there is nothing prissy in the way the social order is defended. The boss has the say-so on everything. Everyone follows the boss, and the boss can oust anyone from their pasture, and has first refusal on water and the lushest grass. All the other horses fall into rank behind him or her (the boss can be a mare).

The boss must always be alert. He knows when danger is near, he decides where to flee to, he defends the herd with his personal intervention. In short, the herd members feel in good hands with their boss. They respect him, and they also trust him implicitly.

To be the boss requires courage and good sense, speed of reactions and experience. Herd leaders have marvellous natural qualities of leadership.

Within the herd, social contact is played out in the form of sniffing, body language and noise. One

Just imagine...

+ It's a lovely, sunny day, and your instructor suggests a ride outside. So you have to lead your horse out of the indoor arena. Beside the exit is a barrel of rainwater, glinting in the sun. You think it's rather pretty, but your horse does not! It snorts in alarm.

+ Because you know that your horse will calm down as soon as it realizes this is only *water*, you remain calm, stand by the barrel and let the horse sniff at the surface of the water. This defuses the situation and the horse, realizing there is nothing to be scared of, quietens down. If you had just pulled it past without being aware of the situation, there would probably have been quite a scene.

sure sign of affection is when two horses groom one another's coats.

Communication for minimalists

Often the slightest twitch of an ear is sufficient for a horse to pass on a message that would have taken us five pages of typescript or a half-hour lecture. The

34

Oh, what an interesting plant.
Let's taste it.
Ouch, it prickles!

highest-ranking animals generally make the least fuss about things. You need to strive to be like this with your horse because it is this that shows you are aware of your supremacy. You must learn to radiate what the others have to work and struggle for. (Do you see how many parallels there are with our human life?) The highest-ranking animals own the greatest individual freedom. They alone decide who may come close to them, when and how close. The rider must take the place of the herd leader in the human-horse relationship, and good groundwork makes that easy to achieve. There are many books on the theme of groundwork that you can use to learn to speak 'Horse'. Don't imagine that this is way beyond you as a student in a riding school. What kind of language do you think school horses speak? Right – 'Horse'.

If that umbrella tries to bite me, I'm off!

From 0 to 60 in 3 seconds

The horse is a flight animal because horses were always a favourite target for predators on the steppes. The only way to avoid being eaten was to recognize the danger quickly, react and scarper. So when a horse takes fright at something, it will still shy, turn around and hurtle away. Until you experience it, you can't imagine how fantastically swift and agile 600kg (1320lb) of body weight can become when it's time to escape from a paper bag fluttering in a bush. You must be aware of this as a rider, and learn to deal with it. To control the deeply rooted flight instinct of the horse, you must learn to take the lead position, that is become the herd leader and win the trust of the horse, so that it will blindly follow you in what it imagines to be dangerous situations. Until that is possible, beginners in particular, who have not yet learned to look after themselves on horseback, will be making regular contact with Mother

Earth. To lengthen these intervals, and make these involuntary landings a rarer event, use the horseback exercises described in later chapters. These exercises should precede group and individual riding instruction. And, to reassure you, you are learning to ride on horses that are already – hopefully – used to overcoming their ancient instincts as far as possible, and that have been trained specially for the purpose of being helpful to you in learning to ride.

Stop, look, listen

If you enable the horse, regularly and in a calm atmosphere, to encounter scary things like umbrellas or plastic sheets, it quickly learns that they pose no danger. If you watch the world through the horse's eyes, you can act in advance and become its equal.

Basic

anatomy

Serious mistakes are often made in posture and in estimating a horse's carrying capacity, owing purely and simply to a lack of knowledge.

As a budding rider, there are certain things that you need to know, so that you can recognize when something is amiss with your partner.

The more you know about equine anatomy and physiology, the more reasonable you'll find the rules of posture on horseback and the standards of riding that your instructor requires. Ask your instructor how and where to feel a horse's pulse, and how best to check his breathing. Start out curious, and stay that way for the rest of your life.

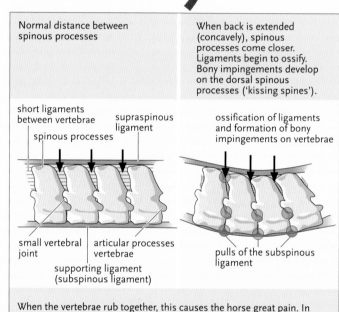

| Normal distance between spinous processes | When back is extended (concavely), spinous processes come closer. Ligaments begin to ossify. Bony impingements develop on the dorsal spinous processes ('kissing spines'). |

short ligaments between vertebrae

supraspinous ligament

spinous processes

ossification of ligaments and formation of bony impingements on vertebrae

small vertebral joint

articular processes vertebrae

supporting ligament (subspinous ligament)

pulls of the subspinous ligament

When the vertebrae rub together, this causes the horse great pain. In extreme cases it even severely limits the mobility of the back.

Focus on the horse's back

All the happiness on earth is found on the back of a horse! Quite right. It is. Ever asked yourself what horses feel about that, though?

Think of your horse's back as a more or less freely suspended bridge construction slung between fore and

Far left: Horses eat most of the time, and rest in between. An enviable lifestyle.

Left: Molly from behind!

Vital statistics

+ An average Warmblood measuring 16 or 17 hands weighs from 500 to 700kg (1100–1550lb) and has 40 to 50 litres (70–88 pints) of blood.

+ The hair of a horse's coat becomes thicker and longer in winter, and this hair thins again in spring – a kind of temperature regulator.

+ In high temperatures, on exertion and under stress or suffering pain, a horse will sweat, particularly on the neck and flanks. Its normal temperature is around 38.5°C (101.3°F), its pulse should be approx. 28–40/minute, and it should breathe on average 12 times a minute.

+ Depending on weather, food intake and physical effort, a horse needs around 40 litres (70 pints) of water a day. A horse's stomach is small in relation to its intestinal volume, and is suited to the intake over many hours of small amounts of food.

+ Horses are herbivores, and have 6 incisors and 12 molars in the upper and lower jaws. The molars grind up food. Horses have a full set of functioning adult teeth by their fifth year. Horses' teeth continue growing throughout their lives.

hind legs. It needs to be stable, indeed almost stiff – so the horse can carry you without health problems – and yet also elastic – so that you can sit on the horse comfortably while it is moving. Sounds like an insoluble paradox, doesn't it? It isn't. By training the horse, its back and the musculature supporting it are strengthened and made elastic, or more flexible, at the same time. By making sure you learn to sit well from the outset, you as a beginner can contribute to this process. One visual indication of a well-muscled back is a spine deeply embedded in the musculature, so that the bones are not the highest point of the back, but sunk below layers of muscle.

If you have the misfortune to start at a riding school where no attention has been paid to training the horses, I feel sorry for you. Your back – and what is at the base of it – will bear painful witness to how uncomfortable it is to sit on a stiff horse with *no* give in its back. But at least you have the choice of never going back; the horse can't escape so easily. Badly ridden horses can even fall victim to serious and extremely painful conditions like so-called 'kissing spines' (see diagram on page 36). Here, the downward curvature of the spinal column forces the dorsal spinous processes against each other, so that they may even rub together. Such a maltreated back can never happily support a rider. Sadly, if a horse holds its head and neck high while being ridden, it will overextend its spine in this way. So you must learn how to ride a horse in a lengthening poise. You can get a feel for this by sitting bareback on a horse and having it stretch its head downwards. You'll feel its back musculature swell beneath you.

A well-ridden horse will have developed sufficient supportive musculature to prevent its back from collapsing. An arched back can also carry a rider without suffering harm.

Basic anatomy · Knowing horses

37

When horses are in pain, they also show it by being unco-operative and bad mannered, or even by bucking and rearing wildly. Many a hair-raising situation could be avoided if beginner riders studied anatomy from the outset, by attending a course or reading up on the subject. If such basic knowledge was widespread, horses would not need to suffer pain. Make it your highest ambition that a horse you are riding does not suffer pain because of it.

A self-experiment: feeling lengthening...

Stand normally upright. Now bend your knees a little and hollow your back a lot, pulling your head right back against your neck. Not pleasant for any length of time is it? Now, though, you have to look at an object directly behind you. You must turn your head as far to the side as it will go in order to look behind you. Ouch! By the time your chin reaches your shoulder, if not before, you can go no further. But you still can't see the object you want to look at.

Now repeat your attempt from another physical position. Stand there again, this time bent slightly forward, with a rounded back and a bent, outstretched, rounded neck. Now try the test of looking round again. Now, you can turn your hips, your whole torso and, because your neck is lengthened, your head, as far as you need to look all the way round, as far as your object or even all the way round to the other side of your body. And this time it didn't hurt.

Your first, painful experience is shared by horses whose backs are not properly engaged, every time they make a turn. It's certainly not pleasant, and repetition is damaging to health.

Only through lengthening work is the horse physically enabled to bear a rider's weight with an arched, freely swinging back, and to achieve other feats of dressage.

... and the madness of the crumpled horse

Another common error among riders is to pull the horse's head with the reins so that it almost touches the animal's chest, then describe the sorry debacle as 'riding on the bit'. Whoever does this has failed to understand an elementary point. A compacted, crumpled horse overextends its back in just the same way as one that is holding its head and neck too high.

Of course, most errors that we humans make with horses are not intentional. Ignorance and superficial thinking are usually to

Head and neck held too high. The back is collapsed and the hindquarters are not under the weight.
This leads to back problems.

Here, the back is arched properly, the horse is lengthening correctly, and its hindquarters are driving it on nicely. It can carry its rider without difficulty.

If martingales or a heavy hand pull the horse into a particular posture, it pulls its back down in response, and the hindquarters are no longer supporting it.

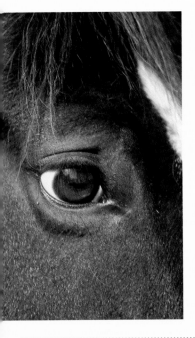

blame. So think, and at least try to understand how some postures can harm a horse in a working situation. Remember this: you too could have been a horse.

Be careful!

Horses have an extremely wide field of vision – almost 360 degrees – thanks to their laterally positioned, widely spaced eyes. Their only blind spots are directly in front

Who can resist this gaze?

of the nose, about a pace away, and immediately behind the croup.

Making the mistake of approaching them through their blind spot, which stimulates a fear reaction in the horse, can create the impression that horses kick out when people walk behind them. This is not the case unless the horse is psychologically disturbed. Please don't creep quickly and quietly around behind a horse like a mouse, but speak to it so that it doesn't take fright. All you need is to say 'Hello there, it's only me' in a friendly tone of voice.

No movement escapes a horse's eye, which is also what causes its great propensity to take fright and flee. This is exaggerated even more because horses do not see particularly sharply, and on the whole they perceive

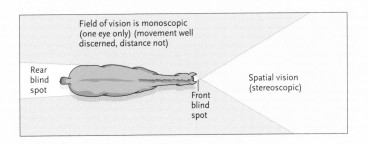

Field of vision is monoscopic (one eye only) (movement well discerned, distance not)

Rear blind spot

Front blind spot

Spatial vision (stereoscopic)

distance poorly. Only in those areas where horses can see with both eyes at the same time is their vision spatial, and therefore sharp. If your horse wants to look at something closely, it must therefore turn its head. Let it do so, because once it understands what is happening, its fear will disappear.

The different fields of vision are governed by different areas of the brain. This is where a particular problem arises: when a horse has seen and accepted something with its left eye, it must learn to accept it all over again with its right eye on the way back. So remember always to consider both sides.

Horses can see well in the dark, and one thing is for sure: to be able to look through a horse's big, gentle

Be a
horse

+ Just to feel the pain of carrying a rough rider, I recommend this exercise. Drop your head and chin so that your chin rests on your breastbone. Now go jogging for half an hour. Two or three minutes will probably be enough to show you what torture it is.

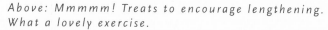

Above: Mmmmm! Treats to encourage lengthening.
What a lovely exercise.

Above right: Mounting from the right – unusual,
but quite possible.

up in the mare's womb. Most horses are left-handed. If the foal is curled up to the left in the womb, the left-hand side of the body is the hollow side. The right-hand side is more used to lengthening. The left-hand side finds it more difficult.

The result of this is that your horse can do a lot of things (eg turns) better on one side than the other, less lengthening side. Now, don't worry. You don't need to write a doctoral thesis about this. But if you understand the basics, you can help the horse to counteract this handicap from infancy, and to lengthen the other side of its body better.

To do this, you need as a rule to work with your horse (if your instructor agrees) on both sides, whether saddling up or mounting. Leading or giving a treat. Don't do everything from the left, but from the right as well, as often as you can. Sometimes technical points will work against you. For example, almost all bridle buckles can only be fastened from the left.

eyes and into its soul is one of the greatest privileges of this world. So allow yourself this privilege, and learn to understand horses.

Favouring one side

What do the Leaning Tower of Pisa and horses have in common? No, not just people taking photographs of them all the time. Asymmetry. This may sound odd to you, because horses look such straight, upright creatures. In fact, instead of talking about asymmetry, I'd rather talk about left- and right-handedness, because asymmetry has such a negative air, suggestive of illness. And what the word expresses is actually quite natural. We humans are born left- or right-handed, and so are horses. It probably has to do with how the foetus curls

Betrayed by a mane

+ Sometimes the way a horse's mane falls indicates whether the animal is left- or right-handed. Usually the mane lies on the 'hollow' side.

Feel free to walk to the horse's right.

It's particularly important to lead a horse from both sides. For one thing, you might find yourself in a situation where a traffic obstacle can only be avoided by being to one side, and for another, it's part of basic groundwork to be able to work with a horse from either side. Apart from handling work on the ground, you can also greatly help the horse to compensate for its favouring of one side by making sure your sitting position is straight and balanced.

Tip

+ If your riding instructor agrees, mount the horse from the right-hand side. Incidentally, you will find this relatively difficult, since it goes against the grain for us (mostly) right-handed humans. All the more reason to try it.

What
hooves
show us

+ Asymmetrical weight-bearing in a horse is clearly seen in the shape of the hooves.

+ If there is no improvement over a period despite professional attention, the problem can probably be ascribed to a fault in the movement apparatus, caused for example by bad influences from the rider, and/or ill-fitting or faulty equipment. In such cases, professionals such as farriers, equine osteopaths and riding instructors need to work closely together with each other and with riders. It is always important to look at any problem in a horse from a holistic perspective.

Sabine Nakelski (farrier)

As you can see, even as a beginner you can be of great help to your horse, if someone will only explain what to do and make you aware of things. Get into the habit of being careful and prudent from the start, otherwise it will be difficult to change your ways later.

Basic skills
to counteract
your fears

Every learner rider gets nervous. My job as a riding instructor is to recognize this fear and its causes by means of communication and body language. I aim not only to pass on theoretical and practical knowledge, but also to consider the mind of the rider, and give confidence, especially to beginners.

Eva-Maria Chiumento (riding instructor, animal psychologist, neuro-linguistic programming practitioner)

Knowledge
undoes fear

Confidence problems can arise both from you trying to improve your prestige in the hierarchy and simply from uncertainty about the horse.

If a horse is reluctant or disobedient while you're riding it, you should analyse how you are feeling, confront your fear and bring it under control.

If you don't quite trust the horse yet, the fears plaguing you will probably run along these lines...

– 'Oh, God, please let me not fall off and hurt myself!'
– 'Please, please, please let the horse not bolt!'

– 'Oh, dear, I hope this monster doesn't stand on my feet!'

Does something strike you? In all three fears, hope is expressed. I have a hope, too. Once you have read this book, and are equipped with everything you need for an enjoyable life in general and riding experience in particular, I hope that you have enormous fun with your horse. It is possible to get to grips with your fears (and, at the same time, those of your horse). You will need a good knowledge of groundwork and the mind of the horse. You'll also have to develop a good sense of balance and excellent reactions. And you'll have to learn riding thoroughly, from the basics up, so that you never lose control over your partner.

You can learn to be a boss

The mind of the horse and the rider's fears are inextricably linked. This is even obvious in everyday activities like catching, leading, tying up and grooming. As a herd animal bound into a hierarchical society, the horse will try again and again to improve its status in relation to you. This process can range from harmless jostling in the stable or during grooming to pretty serious attempts at biting and kicking. It's quite

Just a minute, Swallow, you aren't free to run about in the paddock now, you're working. So, slowly does it, please.

Info

+ Proper, conscious consistency is absolutely fine.

+ On the other hand, being rough or losing your temper with a horse is utterly pointless.

understandable that riders are sometimes afraid when a 600kg (1320lb) colossus kicks up a fuss, with only one flimsy rope, held in trembling hands, to control him. This is why, for your own safety, you must be the boss in this relationship.
Often all that's required to get out of such a difficult situation is for you, the superior animal, to stay calm. Do not allow yourself to be affected by the horse's behaviour. A horse can sense the fear of his rider or groom and, since he constantly seeks protection and safety, as we've seen, if your fear is stronger than his own, he won't feel protected or in good hands. And that will make matters worse. Remember, the horse feels any, even the slightest, shift of atmosphere. There are a number of ways in which you can have a calming influence on the animal in stress situations.

Use your voice

To begin with, your voice is an effective aid, which you're used to using every day as a speaking person. The tone of your voice can communicate the entire spectrum of your feelings. You can sound quiet and loving, you can give praise or reproach, you can be calming, encouraging, decisive and uncompromising, and, the cherry on the cake, you can also sound

magnificently cross, even if you are no such thing. But you should never sink to blustering. We don't want that. In any case, shouting and screaming usually just cover up fear, which the horse will notice at once. So always

Just imagine...

+ You're with your horse, following a field path around the stables. You're leading the horse, as it were taking it walkies.

+ But lying in wait, hanging on a bush, a small piece of red and white ribbon is about to spring out on your horse and rip it to pieces. Well, that's what your horse imagines. You, on the other hand, are quite relaxed, because you have never been attacked by a piece of ribbon.

+ Your calm aura alone will encourage the horse to let its heart beat a little slower, and to walk on for a few more paces in the spirit of 'well, my human is brave, I'll dare to take three more steps'.

+ If you feel the horse hesitate at the last moment to follow you blindly, you can instantly give a calming, but uncompromising order to transform the inner hurricane to a gentle breeze. All you need to say is, 'You can do it, just walk on quietly, I'm here.' And give it a gentle reassuring pat, too.

stay cool, clear and unambiguous, and
communicate what you want to say to your horse in a
friendly and direct way. By the way, you don't need to
restrict this behaviour to horses.
An important sign of possible problems ahead, easy
even for a beginner to recognize, is the freezing or
tensing of a horse's muscles. If your horse senses
something bad, he will literally become rooted to the
spot. It's now your job to get him out of this state,
because next moment he will suddenly explode, and
this is not pleasant (see Just imagine, page 45). Once

Rooted to the spot – just before the explosion?

the situation has eased, you'll see a noticeable
relaxation in the horse's body. He will now follow you,
no doubt a bit crookedly and glancing this way and that,
but he will come.

Talk to your horse!

Never let anyone convince you that there's no need to talk to a horse because they never talk to each other. Not even the last part is true, because horses have a wide repertoire of noises, and can be highly communicative. What is most important for you is to remember that, as a human, you are used to using your voice, and it is a simple and effective means of communication for you to use. Basically, you need have *no* fear of horses. At most, and quite rightly, just a certain respect.

When using your voice as an aid to communication, make sure that you use the same word or sequence of words for defined, constantly repeating instructions – it would be a bit much to ask a horse to learn several foreign languages. Your task in your immediate future as a learner rider is to keep your ears open, so that you hear how more experienced people talk to the horses at your stable. Later, if you'd like to have a horse of your own, it's still vital to keep a clear head about using a consistent vocabulary.

Breathe

Another helpful aid to communication with the horse is your own breathing. Just a brief word of explanation here, because I'll be going into more detail in the practical examples later. Just as horses react with fine sensitivity to changes in voice and atmosphere, they can also perceive changes in the rider's body. And it's no exaggeration to say that they recognize from the slightest breath if you're catching your breath or holding it. There's no harm in starting this work right now: the more consciously you can control your breathing, the easier it will be to learn to ride.

Tips

+ For changes of pace, two-syllable words work best, which is why people say 'Walk on!' and 'Tarrott!' instead of 'Walk!' and 'Trot!' For the horse, the first syllable works as a kind of pre-order, so helping to catch its attention. Some instructors recommend saying something before the actual order, such as 'And now... walk on!' or 'Listen, and... tarrott!'. Try out what works for you, and find out what brings the best reaction out of your horse.

+ Another thing: for active orders and attracting the horse's attention, always use bright, short, clipped sounds. For calming or restraining the horse by using your voice, choose longer, richer sounds.

Stay calm

A rule of thumb for all unpleasant situations is this: stay calm and superior, and do not allow yourself to be infected by any rising panic in your horse. Make an effort to act in a focused and thoughtful way. Acquire as much knowledge as you can, train your powers of observation and your perceptions. When you know what you have to deal with, you'll find it easier to act than if you get nasty surprises. Don't be discouraged. You won't fall off the horse, at least not often, because you'll acquire a good basic technique, and anyway most falls finish with nothing more serious than a couple of bruises and two rather nonplussed faces.

Don't be afraid – you can do it!

Getting to know
horses, instructors and other riders

Your first session should take place in quite an undemanding, relaxed atmosphere, and, in some riding schools, it won't even involve getting on a horse.

There are plenty of important things to be clarified at the outset, and you're sure to have a lot of questions, too.

In an ideal first session, everyone makes themselves comfortable in the tackroom or similar. After an introduction from your instructor you will have the opportunity to explain briefly why they're there and what previous riding experience they have. Then some of the psychological aspects of learning to ride are discussed, and at this point a bit of self-knowledge is called for. Each of you will have to describe your weaknesses and strengths. These questions aren't designed to satisfy the curiosity of the other participants, but to enable the instructor to make the best possible matches in the horse-rider team.

Someone who is fearful and nervous should be allotted an extremely calm school horse. On the other hand, a highly self-confident person might be trusted to pair successfully with a livelier horse.

After the make-up of the future partnerships has been discussed, your instructor should go through what will happen during your first few classes. This will help you to prepare mentally for the experience, so that you arrive at your first 'real' riding lesson in a much more relaxed frame of mind.

No blind dates, please

Next, you should be introduced to your horses, because you need to know who you're going to be working with. The instructor takes you to visit each horse in turn. Don't be afraid to say if you don't like the look of the horse that has been chosen for you. Don't laugh – it's true, the chemistry has to work, and for your first experience or return to the saddle it's really important that everything is weighted as much as possible in your favour. Empathy between horse and rider is just as important as between you and your instructor. It's like a hairdresser – one customer swears by them, the next swears at them.

Stay behind for a while after the introductions and watch everything calmly. There'll be riding lessons next; perhaps you can watch. You know which horse is going to be yours, what his name is and what kind of character he has. Perhaps he will be in the lesson you are watching. You know that you will have to stick to this horse for the first few weeks, because right at the beginning it's important to build up a relationship of mutual trust.

When you come back next week, things will get going in earnest. But by then you'll know the ropes, and you'll fit right in. Have fun!

United we shall never be defeated

In a good school, not only the horses, but also your fellow riders will remain the same, because learning is easier in a small, coherent group. This is much more sensible than elbowing your way anonymously into a load of different riding students, all at different levels of attainment, each week. A better mutual trust builds up, because it is easy for you all to back each other up if you're at the same level.

Unfortunately, many riders have to potter about pretty much on their own. At some stables it's almost frowned upon to ask a fellow rider something – you get the feeling that you shouldn't betray your inadequacies, that 'beginners should be seen but not heard'.

The methods described here are taught in groups of like-minded students, who are encouraged to help one another. All the jobs are practised from every angle. Sometimes you're a rider, sometimes groom, sometimes you're leading, sometimes you're moving poles and barrels, and sometimes you're just a comforter and riding friend. This variety helps all the students.

In a healthy learning atmosphere you'll notice how soon requests and helpful comments start to be bandied around. Rider to groom, 'Could you just adjust the bridle a bit? It's askew.' Rider to other rider, 'You did great with Topsy today.' Do you recognize the holistic spirit? Everyone has a job in this team. People look out for one another, stimulating each other's learning and thinking processes. With a small group, a much wider range of exercises can be completed. Organizing an exercise is much easier for the stable proprietor and instructors if the students are able to help each other, rather than rely on hard-pressed staff, and the students will learn much more, too.

The members of such a group might go on later to buy shares in the same horse, because, after all, they have shared joy and suffering together, which is a nice basis for a lifetime of riding pleasure. It is a lucky horse that finds such a good home.

What do you think, Aztec, shall we make a go of this?

Catching, grooming and so on

Successful riding lessons often depend on what kind of contact you make with your horse when grooming and tacking up.

If you approach your horse in an uninterested or even irritated frame of mind, rush moodily through brushing him, throw the saddle on in a hurry and knock the bit against his teeth while dragging the bridle on, you needn't be surprised if the horse is less than keen to haul you around the countryside on his back. You reap what you sow.

Playing hard to get

If you are asked to bring a horse in from the field rather than simply find him waiting for you in the stable, you might come across a very typical horsey problem. Though they'll never be 'bad', some riding school horses will quite happily show a beginner the limits of their ability if the opportunity arises. Riding school horses can be particularly well practised at trying to avoid work. So, you go up to them in the field and they gladly accept the treat you offer them, thank you, with a playful nudge in the stomach – and then turn around and walk off.

In their wake they leave a bewildered beginner who hasn't got the faintest idea what to do next.

To avoid this situation there should always be an experienced person on hand to supervise bringing school horses in from the paddock.

It's easier in the stable

For the sake of simplicity, then, let's start by approaching the horse in his stable. Open the stable door and say a few friendly words. Now the horse is paying attention to you. He will reach his nose out towards you to have a sniff. Gently place the loosened halter, with calm but decisive movements, over the horse's head.

Goodness, Grandma, what a big nose you've got!

Tip

+ The halter should be made of wide leather or nylon straps. Straps that are too thin can cause serious injury if the horse panics and puts its full weight on the halter.

If the lead rope is already fastened to the halter ring, please don't just let it trail on the ground, otherwise the horse might step on it and in the process jar his neck. Halters come in various designs so check how the one you have in your hands works before you try to put it on the horse. The most simple types just slip over the horse's ears. These are quick to use but you need to be gentle around the ears as some horses find this aspect of being haltered a bit trying. It is often easier to use a halter that has a buckle on the cheek piece. A headshy or otherwise timid horse should only be haltered and tacked up by someone experienced, otherwise his problems will only get worse.

Make sure that all the buckles are correctly fastened, that the halter is not too tight and that it is not sitting too low on the nose or too high over the cheekbone (see photograph, right). When you're ready, tie your horse up in the stable or lead him outside and tie him up there.

Knotting

Proper tying up is a guarantee of the horse's safety and yours. Never tie your horse to something that moves. It has been known for a panicking horse to tear out a stable door to which it was tied. Usually there are iron rings sunk into the wall specially for tying up. If not,

A special
knot

+ For tying up a horse, it is best to use a special safety knot that will undo in a second in an emergency. You only need to pull slightly on one end of the rope to undo it. There are a few ways to tie this knot – this is one particularly neat one: wind the rope end around the post, or through the iron ring, and make a loop with the rest of the rope. Now lay this loop over the rope from behind. Form another loop and thread it through the first, then another, which you thread through the second, and so on up to the end of the rope. If you pull, the rope will undo at once. It isn't a difficult knot to learn – you'll find it easy after a couple of goes.

Knots aren't just for sailors.

make sure that you use a fixed post or something similar.

Don't tie up the horse on too long a rope, otherwise he might step over it, get tangled and panic. Nor should you tie him up too short or too high. The former can cause panic, and the latter isn't good for the horse's back, because it forces it to overextend.

If you have to tie up your horse beside his stable companions, please make sure you leave a safe distance between them. If there are quarrels, the horses might injure each other, and if you are in the way, you might take delivery of a hearty bite that was meant for the next horse.

So, you're sure everything's in order? Great. Now it's time to roll up your sleeves and to go to work, with plenty of elbow grease and the cleaning tools you've brought with you from the tackroom.

Horses can get carried away and groom you too.

Tip

+ If you're pushed for time, confine yourself to the essentials, and clean the hooves and the saddle area. Instead of madly charging through the whole grooming, treat the horse to a few brief but careful strokes to compensate for the lost time.

Grooming and much more besides

Caring for your horse is not just about cleaning. It is indispensable as a trust-building measure and for creating a positive interaction between horse and rider – in the herd, grooming is only seen among horses that get on well together.

Grooming also stimulates the horse's blood circulation, and allows you to examine his body for injuries. Hopefully, too, the pleasant atmosphere that arises when caring for the horse in this way will carry over into the work you do afterwards.

While grooming your horse, you can find out where he particularly likes and dislikes being touched. You can groom his favourite places to make advances in your friendship. Sometimes you'll see a horse hold his head aslant and twist his lower lip in pure pleasure. Don't panic! There's nothing wrong with the horse – quite the opposite. When you find a place that a horse is less happy about, include it in the general routine anyway, being particularly gentle when you do so. You never know when a vet might have to touch a horse in one of these sensitive areas, and you will have made his job much easier through your gentle approach.

Body care made easy

When grooming your horse thoroughly, start at the front end by his throat, and work with circular movements towards the rear through the quarters. This preliminary massage loosens the dirt from the coat and brushes out matted hair. 'Hedgehog' currycombs with small, flexible plastic bristles are useful for this work. They allow you to clean even the bonier parts of the legs and back. Be particularly careful in these areas, though, because they are sensitive. Broad body surfaces should be given a

nice, firm massage – horses prefer this to being touched lightly. Many associate a touch as light as a feather with a fly landing on their bodies, and so they experience it as an irritation. Let your 'feel' and your powers of observation guide you in deciding how gently or firmly to massage and groom. There are no strict do's or don'ts because horses are living creatures, and each one reacts differently. But, once again, it's marvellous training for your powers of observation when you pay attention to what the horse does and doesn't like. If your work is on the right lines, you'll notice above all how the horse becomes more and more relaxed. His head will drop as he stands peacefully, his

Suheila loves the soft brush massage, especially when Stephanie is giving it.

As far as possible, leave the horse's tail and mane alone. If you brush them too much, the horse will lose too much long hair, which only grows back slowly. They need this hair as a protection against insects and the cold. A better plan therefore is to wash the tail occasionally. However, being a riding student, please agree this in advance with the horse's owners. It's generally enough to remove wisps of straw and rough dirt. Do, however, wash the horse's backside from time to time with a sponge. For reasons of hygiene, don't use the same sponge for anything else.

Let's see your feet

All that remains now is to clean out the hooves, and you're done.

Does that make you nervous? No need. The horses you have to deal with as a beginner will be obedient, and practically lift their hooves voluntarily, because they know what to expect from you.

Practise on the horse's left foreleg. Stand to the side by the horse's shoulder, and stroke your hand slowly from his elbow downwards towards his pastern. With many horses, all you need to do is touch the hoof with your finger and they'll lift it. You'll soon learn how much pressure to use, if you start by applying the minimum. However you do it, it's a good idea to use your voice at the same time, saying, for example, 'lift' or 'up'. It is also kind to warn the horse with a friendly 'Hoof down' when you want it to put it back down. At the back, do the same thing. Stand to the side of the horse's leg and

breathing regular. Sometimes the relaxation goes so far that his eyes half close, and he nods off as you busy yourself with getting rid of the dust and dirt.

After dislodging the dirt, you need to brush out the coat. Take the dandy or body brush and work in long, even strokes with the lie of the coat along the horse's body. Clean the brush occasionally by stroking it on the currycomb. The coat is not only being freed from dust and dirt, but it's being shined, so that it starts to gleam. Groom the horse's head with an extra-soft brush. Don't scrub thoughtlessly around the ears, but treat them with special gentleness and care. If the horse learns to enjoy having his ears touched as part of a pleasant stroking experience, he will be less likely to resist when you push the halter over them.

Taking
time...

+ Use grooming time to chat with your horse. Tell him
your thoughts and worries, even share your fears
about your first riding lesson. To your amazement,
you'll see the animal watch you quite calmly as if to
draw all the care from your soul. Horses are
wonderful listeners. They're better people than
people, every time!

Good, no stones or mud in the hoof.

reach down or touch the hoof, and use your voice to
encourage the horse to lift his foot. When he does, rest
the raised leg on your thigh or hold the hoof firmly in
your left hand, your arm going around the front of the
leg. Don't be worried if the horse pulls his leg higher
than you want it, or even stretches it out to the rear.
These are stretching and lengthening reflexes – like
humans, horses have to contend with slight arthritis,
even at a young age. If your horse does this, please
don't struggle madly with his leg, but hold it definitely
but loosely, following its movements. Once he has
finished his stretching, return the leg to where you want
it and continue with the cleaning out.

Use a hoof pick to clean the grooves around the
triangular, spongy frog and the sole of the hoof. Stones
and grit can get trapped here and they can hurt during
work or even cause hoof abscesses if they get further
into the hoof.

Be careful with the metal portion of the hoof pick so
that you don't damage the hoof. An instructor should
supervise your first attempts, and will give you all the
guidance you need.

Saddling

A well-fitted and, of course, well-fitting saddle distributes the rider's weight evenly over the horse's back, and is comfortable for both horse and rider.

So it's important for you as a beginner to know something about how a saddle fits and how to handle it properly. The saddle is usually put on before the bridle. Before saddling up, check quickly under the saddle blanket or numnah. This is to avoid wisps of straw and the like that could irritate your horse's back. At worst, these little irritations can make a horse buck.

Strength in calmness

Before putting on the saddle, make sure the stirrups are run up to the top of the stirrup straps, by the buckles – that is, that they are not hanging loose where they could

BEWARE! Beware!

+ The saddle's centre of gravity should be around the level of the thirteenth thoracic vertebra (approximately one hand's breadth behind the withers). This is also the highest point of the horse's back when, for example, cantering. When removing the saddle, watch out for dry spots in the saddle area (pressure) and also examine the numnah from beneath. Staining from rubbing on the coat and from dust should be even.

+ Any restlessness or unhappiness in the horse while saddling up or fitting the girth points to a problem.

+ If you have checked the fit of the saddle, consider riding faults and physical discomfort in the horse as other possible causes.

Kalle Rehm (equine osteopath and physiotherapist)

Lay the saddle in front of the withers, then slide it back into its correct position.

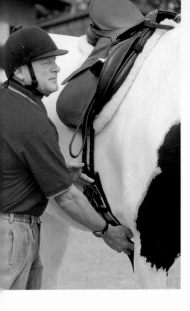

catch your head or hit the horse when you swing the saddle into position. The girth should be lying over the saddle, or pushed safely through a stirrup, again so that it doesn't fly about when you are saddling up.

Stand to whichever side of the horse you like – remember that, in all probability, he will favour his left side. Stroke the flat of your hand down the whole length of the horse's back. Firstly, this lets you feel any scraps of dirt or knots in the coat, which might otherwise cause pressure under the saddle. Secondly, it prepares the horse gently for the arrival of the saddle. Now lay the saddle high up over the withers, and draw it back with the lie of the coat until it is in the right position. A well-fitting saddle should look as if it is moulded in place. Now the deepest part of the saddle is sitting over the horse's centre of gravity, and the withers and loins are free to move. If you miss the right spot, do not be tempted to pull the saddle forwards to correct your mistake, but take it off and start again, going with the lie of the coat. Otherwise, hair rubbing the wrong way under the saddle can cause pressure. Now check to see that the numnah or saddle blanket is sitting straight and even under the saddle. It must not reach over the shoulder blades, and it should not be tight over the spine. Push or pull it up into the gullet of the saddle, back and front, to avoid this. Slip round to the other side under the horse's neck, and check the blanket and girth here too. Then carefully take the girth down, making sure it doesn't knock against the horse's legs, and check underneath the saddle panels to make sure that the girth straps are not twisted.

When fastening the girth, be careful, and initially only tighten as much as necessary to prevent the saddle from slipping. The girth should lie a good hand's breadth behind the horse's elbow joint. So that no skin folds are squashed when fitting the girth, encourage the horse to stretch out his front legs (see photograph, page 56 (top)). This smooths out the skin.

Let the horse get used to the weight of the saddle on his back for a while. Even then, don't fasten it tightly all at once, just bring it up hole by hole. It is best to carry on and bridle the horse and then to walk him around a little before finishing the tightening of the girth, for example once you reach the riding arena. Moving will warm his muscles and relax him.

Your horse will be appreciative if you take it easy when saddling up, and he will let you do your work quite calmly and without disturbance. When you move on to fitting the bridle, make sure you preserve this sense of calmness and relaxation.

Relaxing tummy massage

+ Horses can react sensitively to fitting of the girth. The TTeam method offers a marvellous relaxation exercise, called the Lick of the Cow's Tongue. Using all five fingers and the heel of the hand, stroke from the middle of the tummy upwards towards the back, and repeat. Many horses love this, and it relaxes them for when they have the girth fitted.

Bridling

Although tacking up is not very complicated, it takes time to learn to do competently and in the early stages your instructor will want to oversee what you are doing.

There are always those horses that can be awkward about being tacked up. These must only be saddled and bridled by the instructor or someone equally experienced.

You will usually start riding a horse that has a simple snaffle-type bit, sometimes combined with a flash noseband (see photograph, right), which keeps the bit still in the horse's mouth. I prefer this arrangement because it is more comfortable for a horse that is working with a beginner. No matter how hard they try not to, beginners are liable to unintentionally jab the horse in the mouth because they can't move their hands independently of their seat. Later, when you can control your hands well, you can dispense with the flash. Care should be taken when adjusting any noseband as inhibiting the movement of the horse's mouth is also counter-productive. At the beginning of your riding career, remember the following: fixing the bit until you are secure in the use of your hands is fine, but not lashing the mouth closed! Use this rule of thumb for the various straps on the bridle: you must be able to fit two fingers between the nose bone and the noseband, and

A flash combined with a loose-ring snaffle.

BITS
Bits

+ Even nice, mouth-friendly bits can become instruments of torture in the hands of an insensitive rider.

+ On the other hand, the curb bit can work like the touch of a feather in the hands of someone who knows how to use it.

you should be able to slip your hand easily between the throat lash and the cheek bone.

This is how to bridle a horse. First loosen the halter and take it back over the horse's head so that it hangs around his neck; this means that your horse is still safely tied up, but his head is free to take the bridle. Slip the bridle on as described in the box on the right, do up all the straps, then bring the reins over the horse's head and on to his neck.

Later, removing the bridle should be done just as carefully. Your movements need to be slow and well thought out, so that the bit does not jar against the horse's teeth as he drops it out of his mouth. Never drag the headpiece down over the ears, but carefully pull it forward over them, allowing it to slide slowly down the nose bone. Meanwhile, leave the reins hanging across the horse's neck, so that no one can step on them, and you still have the horse under control, even without its bridle on.

Tips

+ On a Saturday afternoon, come to the stable and polish your horse's saddle and bridle until they gleam. This will be educational for you, and the riding school staff will love you for it.

+ Ask your instructor to show you how to fit the bit in the horse's mouth. The cheek pieces should hold it high enough to create a small 'smile' on the horse's lips.

Step by Step
Tacking up

1 Standing face forward beside your horse's head, hold the bridle firmly in your right hand. Using your left hand, place the bit in front of the horse's lips.

2 Using the pressure of your left thumb between the horse's lips or in the bars of the mouth, encourage your horse to open his mouth. At the same time, raise the bridle and slip the headpiece over his ears.

3 Gently and carefully, bend the ears backwards or forwards so that the headpiece goes easily over them. Carefully pull the forelock through so that it is outside the browband, and check that everything is level. Now fasten the throat lash.

4 All straps must sit flat against the horse's head. Remember – not too tight, not too loose. Tightly lashed nostrils through which a horse can hardly breathe are just as bad as a browband that is so loose that you could push a football through it.

Learning to lead in the
stable,
riding arena and countryside

When leading a horse, remember his past as a herd animal of the open steppes.

In the herd, it's the boss who decides how close another horse can get and the boss will never allow himself to be overtaken. In this case, you are the boss, and the horse must remember to keep a certain distance away from you, and to recognize your leadership role.

Even experienced horses that have already learned to be led must always be led correctly, because even riding school horses will sometimes decide that they don't want to do as you ask, and if you don't have the right attitude you won't even get out of the stable, let alone to

Tip

+ The horse must recognize you as the boss. This is for your safety and the horse's. When you want to get several hundred kilograms of body weight, backed up by enormous power, to go somewhere with you, your muscles are of little use. You need technique.

Very good, Stephanie, that's the way to hold Suheila in any situation.

the riding arena. Groundwork on the different leading positions is a subject in itself, and there is plenty of excellent literature on it.

Some leading know-how

· Never lead the horse on the halter or headcollar alone. Always use some kind of lead rope, even over the shortest distances. This rope must neither be too long nor too short. Imagine the horse takes fright. If the rope is too long he can really get going before you have a chance to pull him up, which means he will pull away; too short and he will give your shoulder a nasty jolt, your instinct then is to let go – and then he's off again.

· Keep a set distance between you and the horse. This is important. If he is right at your heels or your shoulder, it makes it much too easy for him to barge you, and if he takes fright, he could easily knock you down.

· The horse's head must not overtake your shoulder. In the herd, animals of higher status do not allow this to happen.

· Hold the rope loosely and not too close to the headcollar, so that you can let it out when you need to. If you're to the horse's left, it's best to hold the rope in your right hand and catch the end in your left. If you're on the other side, reverse this. Never wind the rope round your hand. If the horse pulls away unexpectedly, you might break your hand or find you are dragged along the ground because you couldn't let go in time. Ouch! Do not look the horse in the eye as you walk off, but look in the direction you want to go. And remember to use your voice.

· Never hold the rope under tension, or taut, as you walk. It should hang down a little, but it must never be so long that the horse or you might trip on it.

Trust is good – control is better

Whenever you are leading a horse be aware of the possibility of something happening to upset the applecart. Then if he does decide to join his fellows in the field, or make a beeline back to his stable, you are ready and can react quickly. Keep watch out of the corner of your eye to see if your partner is about to give you the runaround.

Concentration is the key; never absent-mindedly let the horse traipse along behind you. The job of being boss is highly demanding, because you must be constantly alert.

If your horse tries to come closer to you, urge him away by shaking the rope and sending pulses down it. If he tries to overtake you, strike him briefly on the chest with the rope end, or give a quick sharp admonishing tug on the lead rope.

When you are leading a horse past stables or other horses that are also being led, keep your eyes open. In a narrow stable yard a stabled horse might take the opportunity to give your charge a nip on the backside. You are there to protect your horse in this situation, so make sure it doesn't happen. Otherwise he will be very disappointed that he is being good and following you, and his reward is to get bitten. Ask for help from other

Always in proportion

+ With horses, the level of any 'orders' you give is always dictated by the situation and the temperament of the horse. When safety is a concern, stronger measures are justified.

people if necessary. As usual, teamwork is a great help, so don't be shy to ask.

Going to the riding arena

These rules also apply when you're leading your tacked-up horse from his stable into the indoor school. In this case, though, the lead rope is replaced by the reins, which should be taken over the horse's head. Lead the horse gently and calmly to the mounting block. Do not pull him along by the reins as this will be very uncomfortable and will make the bit rattle against his teeth or pull it through his mouth.

Because you have to do it so much – leading to and from the stable, to and from the field and so on – you will find that you learn how to lead quickly and it can be fun. Once you're more advanced in your training, and are perhaps allowed to take the horse for a walk on your own, I can promise you that this is balm for your soul. Talk a lot to your partner, and your next riding session will be a joy.

Left: Stephanie learns about bareback riding, while Peter learns how to lead.

Below: Leading gives confidence to learner riders.

Leading in the country

There are a few things to remember when leading in open country. If you're just going for a simple walk with a well-behaved horse, you can safely do so with just the halter and rope. If you are leading a ridden horse, your lead rope will be attached to the noseband or bit ring, and the rider can also influence the horse by using the reins.

On roads, you and the horses are road users. Do not expect too much consideration from motorists. To protect yourself, your fellow riders and the horses, make sure you do the following:

– Make eye contact with the driver, and make clear hand signals telling him what to do.

– Stay friendly no matter what happens. Losing your temper achieves nothing, except to make the horses more nervous. If in doubt, forget that it is your right of way and yield to the car, just to get rid of it. It's better to run the risk of muddy or wet feet than to risk your life or someone else's.

– If a driver's actions constitute a danger, note the registration number and follow this up afterwards. But

Top right: When you've done some good work in the riding arena, it is wonderful to go and relax in the country for a while.

Bottom right: Whether you're riding or leading, as a road user you must always behave correctly.

aim to keep the atmosphere within your group of horses calm and relaxed.

- Lead and ride horses on the same side of the road as if you were driving a vehicle. As a group, even if there are several of you riding together, you must stay on one side of the road.
- If you have to cross a road, always do it as a group. If only one horse crosses and the others become disturbed by this, the consequences can be disastrous.
- The first and last in the group have important jobs to do as scouts. If a vehicle approaches from ahead, the first shouts, 'Careful, tractor coming!' The last does the same.

During these walks, you can talk shop with your instructor and your fellow riders, or practise various skills. The horses will also enjoy this, because walking together in a nice group of cheerful people is a wonderfully relaxing thing to do. Now you're perfectly equipped for riding out with a team of horses in the not too distant future. Notice something? Bit by bit, you're getting closer to your dreams.

And so,
on to
the horse!

You've done it. Your horse is fully tacked up and his coat has been polished until it shines. All being well, he's in a good mood, and he's standing in front of you. Now it's time to get to develop a feel for your position as a rider – with and without a saddle.

On a bare back –
not for nudists

'All well and good', you're thinking, gazing at the horse's smooth back. 'But how do I get up there without stirrups?'

Be positive, but land gently on the horse's back.

Don't worry, you'll scale the heights with the help of a mounting block, stool or step ladder. And I have talked so much about self-knowledge being a decisive character trait for successful riding, well, you can use that here as well.

For the sake of the back of whoever's helping you, please be honest about how much you weigh. Whether or not you're using a saddle, always try to land smoothly

and softly on the horse's back. Just imagine what it might be like to have 60–80kg (130–180lb) suddenly crash-land on your back. Your instructor will be holding the horse on a halter and rope. So you are in safe hands, and you can tackle the exercises quite calmly.

Now, how does it feel? It's nice to touch the horse's soft, warm coat and the sense you get of its power and muscles is amazing.

Up at last

Now that you're sitting up there, quietly find your bearings. Greet your horse. Stroke the horse's neck, scratch his mane and just feel comfortable. Now bend forward over the horse's neck (see the photograph on page 65). Let your arms hang down to either side of his shoulders, and rest there. Horse skin smells good. Lay your cheek against his neck and have a good cuddle. Now straighten up slowly again, and sit loosely.

The next exercise demands a bit more courage. You're going to turn round until you are sitting backwards, facing to the rear down the horse's croup. Take one leg up over the horse's neck to the side. Be careful – if your hip joints crunch, you've taken it up too high. You're now sitting sideways. You need balance here, and this is the first time you've practised getting it in your new riding career.

Don't worry, you're training in a team, and your fellow riders will support you if you feel doubtful. And everyone can listen to the instructor's corrections for themselves, and learn from them. Now take a leg once more over the horse's croup, and you're sitting backwards. Butterflies in the stomach? Not necessary. Now lie quite flat with your upper body on the horse's back and croup (see photograph on page 68). Your

An interesting perspective!

head to one side. Your legs and arms hanging loosely and relaxed down the horse's sides. This should be wonderfully pleasant. Close your eyes and think of nothing for a moment.

Just feel. If you place the flats of your hands against the horse's stomach, you can feel his breathing. His body is warm and soft, and occasionally it rocks gently as the horse moves, now relieving one hind foot, now the other. You feel quite nice and relaxed up here. Where did your fear go?

After a while, straighten up again and use the same procedure as before to turn yourself round to sit forwards on the horse. Sadly, you must now slide down off the side of the horse – which is also not as dramatic an experience as you expected – because it's the next person's turn. Remember to say a friendly goodbye to the horse before sliding off and thanking him. Putting up with this behaviour with such good humour is worth a few kind words and a gentle stroke.

Left: Just wake me in 20 minutes or so.
Below: Three hours across the prairie? Margaret wouldn't hold out like this.
Bottom: Right, Michael, now just slide off.

The
sack of flour

+ The name of this exercise is not intended as an insult. It's just named after what it looks like.

+ Lie on your front across the horse's back, in the position always used by cowboys in Westerns to transport captured cattle-rustlers. To get into this position, you'll probably need the help of your fellow team members. Take time to get balanced.

+ Once you feel secure, let your legs, arms and head hang down quite relaxed. This is a wonderful exercise for promoting the circulation of blood to the brain. After a short while come back up again – but slowly, to avoid dizziness. Sit upright, then sideways on the horse, then simply slide down. For the sake of your joints, land softly whenever you come off the horse.

Sensory training
without the saddle

Now that you've tried such daring exercises on horseback, you'll have no problem being led on a walking horse.

Once again, you're sitting on the horse's bare back, because that's the best way to accustom yourself to the movements of the horse beneath you and to distinguish between them. The closer you are to the horse, the better. In every pace, there is a definite sequence of steps, in other words, the hooves are lifted and set down in a particular order. Once you are an accomplished rider, you will be responsible for exercising your horse correctly, so you must learn to feel when a horse has come off his left or right leg, and which hoof is in the air, in order that you can learn to give the correct aids to stimulate the horse into further activity.

Info

+ Most riding schools offer little or no sensory training.

+ But sensory training is wonderful in that it offers beginner riders in particular a great opportunity to accustom themselves more quickly to the horse's movements.

Close your eyes... and enjoy

To begin with, close your eyes, because this heightens your other senses. You'll quickly understand how wonderful it is to concentrate only on the pleasant rhythm of movement. Because your eyes are shut you can't be distracted by what is going on around you and your attention is focused inwards not outwards. Sit completely relaxed and allow yourself to be carried. Your upper body is upright, and your legs are lying loosely around the horse's ribcage. Your heels point down. Firstly, let's work a little on your seat using elements of the Feldenkrais method to harmonize you internally so that you get an image in your mind of your posture, which you will then come to take up quite naturally when on the horse. (Moshé Feldenkrais, 1904–1984, spent a lifetime exploring the relationship between consciousness and movement. His work has helped many people, from actors and musicians to those with cerebral palsy and other neurological disorders.)
In order to straighten your somewhat forward-bent torso and raise your slightly downward gaze, and to get your legs down a bit, please imagine the following: your riding hat suddenly becomes very light. Much lighter than it really is – you have the feeling that a bird wants to carry it off in flight. But the bird is only helping you. It flies with you over the horse, lightening your head, neck and torso. Now you share this work of lightening, you're as light as a feather. Straighten up, stretching yourself up at the same time towards the bird. Lovely.
Never lift your knees upwards while sitting on the horse.

To make your legs longer, we're going to attach imaginary bricks to your feet. Breathe evenly and calmly, and concentrate only on the feeling of the heavy stones on your feet. See, now you have a nice seat. Take every opportunity to repeat these visualization exercises. Be creative. You'll be amazed how much of an influence this sort of mind-bending has on your riding.

At first, all these exercises should be done at walk, and nicely relaxed. For now, that's still the only pace in which you won't automatically clench your legs and start to become cramped. You will soon start to learn about the other paces – trot and canter – too but in good, safe hands, on the lunge.

Feel it...

Now that you're sitting nice and loosely, you can start to learn how to feel the sequence of steps a horse takes as he walks. To make it easier, in most schools, your horse will be led over poles on the ground, which emphasizes the movement. As he moves his legs, you will feel your hips moving and rotating slightly in sync with him. They don't only move up and down, but also forward and back. The hip is a ball-and-socket joint, so its movements are highly flexible. See if you can feel when one leg feels tighter on the horse's ribs than the other.

Left: Stephanie is concentrating fully on the movement of the horse.

Below: You feel more with your eyes closed.

Digression: the
basic paces

To be able to influence the horse's movement, a rider must also understand it thoroughly.

Here is a theoretical explanation of what you will discover in practice during the course of your sensory training.

The walk...

is a movement in quadruple time, where the legs are moved in diagonal succession and at regular intervals. For example, the sequence is right fore, left hind, left fore, right hind, and so on.
At a normal pace, the hind feet should more or less step into the prints left by the front feet.
If the horse swings both legs on one side forward at a time, eg left fore and left hind, and plants both feet simultaneously, this is called an amble or stepping pace gait. This sequence of steps is rare in most horses and would be regarded as a false gait in them, but in many gaited horse breeds it is desirable.

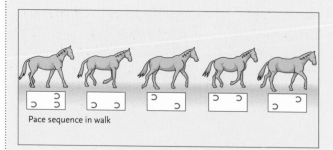

Pace sequence in walk

The trot...

is a sequence of steps following each other in double time. Two diagonal legs are moved forward and brought down simultaneously. Thus left fore and right hind or right fore and left hind move together. Between these steps is a period of suspension in which one pair of legs is being lifted as the other is being brought down.

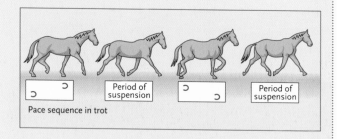

Period of suspension   Period of suspension

Pace sequence in trot

The canter...

is a sequence of skips in triple time, each followed by a period of suspension. The rhythm is pa-da-dam (suspension), pa-da-dam (suspension), pa-da-dam (suspension) and so on. It almost looks as though the horse is cantering on an arc through the air.
– First phase: forequarters up – weight on lowered hindquarters – only one hind foot bearing weight.

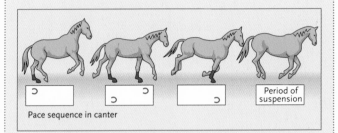
Pace sequence in canter

– Second phase: horizontal – weight on diagonal leg pair, one fore and one hind leg.
– Third phase: landing on one fore foot – this foot bears all the weight.
– Fourth phase: all four feet in the air – period of suspension.

After this, the sequence repeats from the front. The fore and hind feet are not planted next to each other. The feet of one side reach further forward. This is the meaning of the expressions 'left lead' and 'right lead' canter.

Notes:

+ Walk-paces – Quadruple time

Counting along: 1 – 2 – 3 – 4 / 1 – 2 – 3 – 4

Trot-steps – Double time

Counting along: 1 – 2 / 1 – 2

Canter-skips – Triple time

Counting along: 1 – 2 – 3 / or pa-da-dam

You can practise and memorize the rhythm nicely by sitting on the horse in each gait and counting along aloud, just like in a dance class.

This is an important feeling because once you can get this you can start to use your legs to move the horse on in walk. The horse's ribcage will press alternately against each leg as he walks. The feeling is created by the horse bringing a hindleg forward to take a step – his stomach muscles follow this process. At the exact moment you feel the movement against your leg, you can squeeze that leg against the horse to encourage him to tread more energetically and bring his hind hoof further under his centre of gravity.

Feeling the rhythm in yourself

During this exercise, it helps your concentration on feeling the rhythm in yourself if you say aloud, 'Now, now, now', as you feel the movement of the horse. Don't be disappointed if you can't feel it at once, or not at all. All riding is a matter of practice, and the more often you have the opportunity to feel and practise, the better.

A very useful exercise is to be led through a zigzag made of ground poles. The turns that the horse has to make to negotiate this maze will give you a first feeling of how his body bends. Your sense of balance and your reactions will be trained, because you must always be ready to follow his movements softly. These sensory exercises are a wonderful way of becoming used to these unaccustomed movements, but also of building your own trust in the horse. When you open your eyes once more, you'll feel as if you're on another planet. Please remember these lovely, relaxing exercises, and try to repeat them whenever you can. Even – and perhaps especially – when you've been riding for years.

Exercises with
saddle pad *and* girth

Now that your first contact with a horse's back has given you a positive introduction, let's go on with some more training.

To begin with, you'll be working nice and gently on a still horse, with an assistant standing beside his head, then you'll repeat some of the exercises while riding. These exercises are designed to build up your confidence so don't get worried about them. You will improve your sense of balance, your reactions, the mobility of your limbs and your co-ordination, all at the same time and all in an enjoyable way.

No risk, no fun!

This time, a well-upholstered saddle pad or blanket is fastened to the horse's back using a special girth called a surcingle. This will protect the horse's back and cushion it against small pressure points, such as knees and feet, because of course you don't want to hurt it. The point of these kneeling and standing exercises is to learn about weight distribution and balance.

Let's start with kneeling on the horse. After greeting your horse warmly, begin by sitting on him, keeping your upper body light and relaxed. Now draw both thighs up across his back, supporting yourself with both hands on the surcingle, until you are kneeling on him. Your knees are close together, the soles of your feet pointing outwards. Never stretch your joints out completely, in this or any of the exercises described here. When you do this exercise while the horse is walking, the gentle flexing produced through the knee and hip joints being free to move is absolutely essential. Your hands are still holding the surcingle, but now you should feel confident enough to let go, and to rise up a little higher. Spread your arms out to the sides, and congratulate yourself on reaching a little further. It will benefit your sense of balance now to try a few exercises turning from the hips with outstretched arms. Give it a go, it's not that difficult.

Christine is kneeling, arms outstetched, nice and loosely on a very relaxed Millie.

The icing
on the cake...

...and you're the cherry on top!

+ In preparation for this exercise, your instructor will tie a rope onto a ring between the grips on the surcingle. Now, quite slowly, 'sit' on the soles of your feet, keeping hold of the grips on the surcingle.

+ Stand up, keeping your knees slightly bent and using the rope for support. Many beginners, overwhelmed by their own courage and the wonderful view up there, throw their arms in the air. Feel free to do so! If you start to totter, drop quickly on to your knees and take hold of the grips. But what can go wrong? To left and right, someone is there to catch you, and they will hold the horse, who is perfectly composed anyway.

I'm sure you didn't expect to be able to stand on top of the horse before you even learned to ride, did you?

In this sequence (starting left) Margaret has stood up beautifully, and now she executes a neat and courageous leap down from Millie, to much applause.

Exercises with saddle pad and girth   And so, on to the horse!

76

Please remember that, when you come back down on the horse's back, you must never do so heavily or roughly, because if this happens often, even a good-tempered and well-trained school horse will become fed up. Always balance your body weight using the surcingle, and sit down slowly and smoothly. This strengths the musculature of your arms and back, and keeps the horse happy in his work.

Exercises on (moving) horseback

You can do the same exercises on horseback while the horse is moving as when he is standing still. This training on a moving horse is wonderful for your sense of rhythm and orientation. It trains many muscle groups, and makes the whole body work. While you are doing the exercises, the horse is usually walked at a steady and even pace in a big circle on a lunge rein. For a nervous rider, however, it is possible to have a someone leading the horse at his head, to provide just a little more confidence.

Now the thought will occur to you, how do I get on while he is moving? A ladder on wheels? Motorized plastic stools? Nope. You walk alongside the horse's girth, matching his pace and with an assistant beside

No worries

+ Horses specializing in horseback exercises are usually well trained, and trust the voice of the lunge leader even in supposedly precarious situations. This is also your chance to practise the use of your own voice and body to influence the horse.

you. You take hold of the surcingle in both hands. Count in the rhythm of the horse's steps: 'One, two, three, jump!' At 'jump', jump up – your assistant will also grab you and push you up. Between your pulling power and the assistant's bunk-up, you will get on board and land gently. This mounting exercise is a lot of fun, which is what riding is all about.

One of the first exercises that I like to do with beginners is called the 'Mill' (see page 77). This develops your sense of balance, the flexibility of your hip joints, the elasticity of your legs and the strength of your abdominal and thigh musculature.

I also like to give newcomers a first taste of a canter on the lunge. If you have grips (on the surcingle) that you can hold on to, you'll feel really secure and probably never want to stop. And if you close your eyes, you can imagine that you're riding your horse alone through meadows and fields...

Exercising with someone leading, you can learn to feel the horse's movements safely, in good hands.

Completely
detached...

+ The 'Mill' is a 4-phase exercise in which you turn through 360 degrees by taking one leg at a time over the horse's neck and backside. It teaches you to observe the pace rhythm of the horse, to shift your weight as you sit sideways, and to use your hands dextrously and skilfully in order to take hold of the surcingle grip at the appropriate moment.

There are many exercises to make your learning exciting. They are lots of fun for all participants, and can also be integrated again and again into more advanced training procedures. Here the horse wears draw reins which are attached to the surcingle between his legs. They act as an additional control on the horse's head.

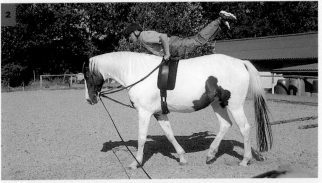

An exemplary stretch forwards of the leg for the 'Mill'.

1 *Roland in an almost perfect 'Flag' exercise...*
2 *... developing momentum for the vault...*
3 *and jumping sideways off the horse!*

Exercises with saddle pad and girth   And so, on to the horse!

77

And down we go

You can never completely exclude the possibility that some time in your riding career you're going to take a tumble. It happens from time to time, even to professionals.

There are, however, plenty of exercises you can do to ease the process of falling, and to overcome your fear and insecurity in advance. Many falls result in nothing more serious than a couple of bruises and a nasty shock. However, fear can make falling more likely because of what it does to the rider's body, making the muscles tense up. If the horse shies, you won't be able to follow the movement if you're tense. And the result is you in an undignified heap on the ground.
In the past, falling was regarded as inevitable but little was done to prepare riders for how to fall and how to avoid falling. Nowadays you can take courses in falling! Highly recommended.

A stitch in time saves nine

Things you can practise at home are turning somersaults, rolling backwards and forwards, rolling into a ball like a hedgehog. Don't use your hands to support yourself, but keep them in against your body. Dare to fall out of bed. But please cushion the floor well first.
Sit, blindfolded, on a stool or a beach ball and let someone you trust push you off without warning. Don't do this on a stone floor – make your landing as soft as

possible with an exercise mat. The more often you practise, the sooner you'll get rid of your fear of crash landings. A horse is considerably higher than a stool or a ball, but practising rolling out of a fall will help you a great deal when the real thing happens.
Children still have a natural hedgehog instinct, and are also much more agile when they fall. They fall more often and more happily. Adults, on the other hand, have to retrain themselves, but it is possible to have fun in the process.

You can do stretching exercises wherever you are – but please don't forget to warm up first.

Learning how to fall

Practice will prove to you that dismounting a horse in an unconventional fashion isn't all that dramatic. Your greatest fears lurk in your imagination, where you picture yourself falling from a height of three metres (10 feet) and being pulped by gigantic hooves. I can set your mind at rest here, because even the biggest breed of horse, the Shire, only reaches a stick measure (the height of the withers) of about two metres (6½ feet). However, some exercises before your riding (or falling) lesson are a good idea. You should loosen up a bit before any kind of physical exercise, because well-warmed-up, stretched muscles can react much more quickly without being hurt.

Also try to do the turning exercises that have already been described. These are the best way of fighting fear on horseback. Especially as they are done on a horse that is well trained for this kind of instruction, so you can concentrate fully on the exercises.

Your arms won't get any longer than that, so let go, Stephanie. You can do it.

Have a go...

– Dismounting a different way
Sitting on the horse's smooth back, slide gradually backwards along the croup. As long as your arms reach, keep a hold on the surcingle grips, then creep farther back, with the flats of your hands on the horse's back. Now just let yourself slip off backwards over the tail. Lo and behold! You're down. It wasn't as high as you expected, and it's a new perspective. Well done. Try again straight away.

– Dismounting as if you were leaving the saddle
Sit normally, lift your right leg and swing it over the horse's back, and slide off. Use the grips, that's what they're there for.

– If you're feeling a bit more sure of yourself, do the same exercises again, with a bit more 'oomph'. Or try jumping off with a careful 'Flank' – another standard from the world of horseback exercises:

From an upright seat, get some real momentum going in your legs. Lean your upper body easily forward, and bring your legs up and over the horse's back. Support yourself on the grips with your hands. Once both legs are in the air, it's easy to turn your hips towards the lunge leader and jump sideways with your legs together to dismount. Be careful when landing: remember to cushion the movement softly with your feet, knees and hip joints. Never land with straight legs. That would do your joints no good at all.

– It's a great idea to do the Flank exercise at a trot. This time, you land running along in the horse's rhythm – now you know why jogging was recommended as conditioning training earlier on. As soon as your feet touch the ground, start to run along with the trot. For balance, once again do use the surcingle grips. This exercise will also show you, for situations where you are in danger of toppling off the saddled horse, that it's possible to stay on your feet and keep yourself together. It may well sound complicated, but in practice it's quite simple, and a lot of fun.

Once you've dismounted voluntarily at a trot a few times, you'll also find that the idea of falling has lost some of its terror.

Fear under control

These dismounting exercises are also suitable for when you're riding in the saddle with someone leading you. They aren't as easy as when you do them bareback, but the experience is effective, because it's very close to riding reality.

Of course, the idea is to stay on the horse as much as possible. But since pride comes before a fall, no one should imagine that they are immune to the possibility. It's good to be somewhat prepared for the occasion, and it follows that being prepared will dilute a lot of your fear. If you have an idea of what to expect, it's not half as bad. So let yourself fall. There'll always be someone in your life to catch you.

Mounting to conserve energy

✚ Normally, for horseback exercises, you jump up on to the horse, and after a couple of attempts, this will probably leave you out of breath. So use a plastic stool or something similar for mounting. Climb up on to this, and mount the horse from there.

Angi meets
Brandy, Whisky & Co.

Angi Johnson (remember her?) is proud as a peacock. After more than a year's break from riding – for reasons I hardly need to explain (see page 13) – she's plucked up courage again. Hurrah! A new beginning. Together with a girlfriend, she's going to the country to take a weekend riding course for beginners. They'll stay at a bed and breakfast on the edge of the village. Two hours of instruction daily, and one hour of theory. Sounds good. No sooner said than done and booked.

At least there's plenty of light in the training stable, even if most of it is coming from fluorescent tubes, and there are hordes of people helping with grooming and saddling up.

Amazingly, Angi is only a tiny bit afraid. Somehow, she feels that things can't possibly go worse than they did the first time. Poor Angi, how wrong we can be.

The training horse allotted to her is not too big, and he's also quite friendly. At least he hasn't bitten or kicked her yet. Bill Brown, the riding instructor, in the prime of life, strolls through the stable, whistling happily. Angi murmurs humbly, 'Nice that you're in such a good mood, it makes me feel better before we've even begun.'

Bill Brown explodes in a roar of laughter (not the last time Angi will hear this) and gurgles, 'Weekenders are my favourites!' He smiles away down the lane.

Angi has a quick look to see what the name is on the door to her horse's stall. Ah. Brandy, he's called. Interesting. Passing by on the way to the riding arena, she reads the other names out of the corner of her eye. Whisky, Vermouth, Absinthe. A still, small voice deep inside Angi begins to clear its throat. Be quiet, she orders it, and enters the arena.

Things are on the move here. There are more than ten trainee riders, who are going to ride together. Bill Brown waits until everyone has mounted – for which much thanks – and then he's off.

'We're forming a group, Snowball at the front, at a working tempo, waaaaaalk ON!'

Just a minute! Angi recognizes that tone of voice. She takes a last, longing look at her as yet undamaged fingernails, and the horse trots on. After a few seconds, as if following a secret command, Brandy leaps to the side, and Angi reacquaints herself with the ground. Bill slaps himself vigorously on his enormous thigh, and bawls, 'Dear, oh dear, oh dear, there's Brandy up to his usual tricks again! Didn't hurt, I hope! Well, there you go, that's riding for you. Can't call yourself a rider if you haven't fallen off.'

Angi bravely pulls herself together, and climbs – stiff as a board with fear – back on to Brandy's back. I need hardly tell you that later Whisky, Vermouth et al also get up to their usual tricks. Each of the horses is in possession of a hilarious box of comic turns – according to Bill Brown, who, it turns out, is licensed to dispense the drinks in the tackroom.

Poor Angi – keep looking!

Where's the ladder?
Mounting and dismounting

At last you've got this far. Foot in the stirrup, swing up!

Hang on, not so fast. Mounting from the ground can hurt the horse, because for an instant your whole body weight is hanging on one side of the saddle, pulling the opposite side tightly against the horse's sensitive shoulder blade. The sideways pressure, which the poor horse can do nothing about, twists the shoulder uncomfortably. It must be a horrible feeling, and yet the horse is expected to stand still until the rider is seated. Smaller horses are easier and quicker to mount than large ones, and you see practised riders swing easily and nimbly into the saddle. But there's never any harm in using an aid to mount – it makes it easier on you and on the horse – and take no notice if people are inclined to laugh at you for it. One day they will realize that you are right. Let's hope it is sooner rather than later. There will always be situations in which you simply have no choice other than to mount without help. So every

rider must be able to do so, and once you are happy getting on and off using a mounting block, you should occasionally practise getting on from the ground. However, what is so wrong, in normal, everyday situations, with making things as pleasant as possible for the horse? And for you too. Especially for the inexperienced newcomer – namely, you.

Using a mounting block

Most horses are happiest being mounted from the left-hand side – remember what was said earlier about one-sidedness? So position the horse to the left of the mounting block and then stand on the block facing the horse. Hold the reins in your left hand and put your left foot into the stirrup. Then, with your right hand resting on the back of the saddle, hop with your right foot and spring up into the saddle (see also page 84).
Practise getting on from the horse's right-hand side as well. Remember to reverse the procedure described above – put the reins in your right hand and your right foot in the stirrup then swing your left leg over the horse's back.
It's important to keep watching the horse's head as you get on so that you can gauge what he is thinking. Look at his ears, too. This will give you some warning about his state of mind. Don't get on if he looks like he is about to set off in fright. Remember 0 to 60 in three seconds? Calm a fidgety horse down before you mount. Remember too that, as a beginner, you should ask your instructor or a team colleague for help if you feel you

Info

+ You already know something about horses favouring one side, like our left- and right-handedness. Always mounting from the same size reinforces the negative aspects of this asymmetry in horse and rider. Working more flexibly is good for you both.

need it. They can counterweight the saddle, in other words, lean their body weight on the free stirrup on the opposite side of the saddle at the moment when you mount, to keep the saddle in its correct position and minimize the pressure on the horse's withers.

Above: Chelsea stands patiently still until Stephanie has mounted.
Right: Make life easy for you and the horse.

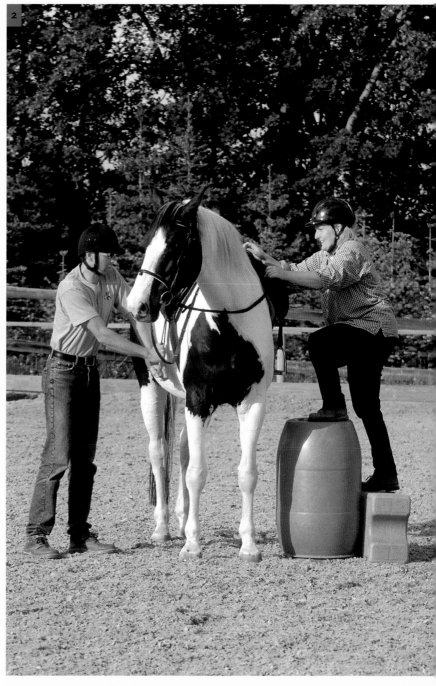

Step ^{by} Step

Mounting

1 When mounting, keep hold of the reins, so that the horse is under control throughout. Place your foot in the stirrup.

2 Use your other hand to grip the back of the saddle and push yourself off the mounting block with your foot. Remember that you must land in the saddle slowly and as lightly as a feather. Once you are in position, calmly arrange the reins and stirrups.

3 You should have already fixed the approximate stirrup length from the ground.

4 If anything does need changing, someone will help you at this early stage in your riding career. Only ride off when everything is in order. This is also a good exercise for the horse's obedience. Just as you must practise mounting patiently, so must your horse.

5 This method of mounting is not to be recommended, even for experienced climbers.

Feet back on the ground

Similar rules apply to dismounting. First, find a quiet place in the centre of the riding arena, usually parallel to the middle line. Halt your horse and let him stand so that you both relax. With a friendly 'That was nice!' and stroking your horse, say goodbye while taking both feet out of the stirrups and lifting one leg back over the saddle – it's up to you which side you choose to dismount. Now slowly slide down the horse's side, and land gently on the ground with flexion in your knees. Take care not to land on the ground with too much force, then your joints will come to no harm dismounting. If you feel a little stiff from being on the horse wiggle your feet around a little to get the blood supply moving before you dismount.

If you have any spare time left, you can entertain the wooden horse for a few minutes with your mounting and dismounting practice. Don't forget to give it a carrot.

A word about gadgets

Depending on where you learn how to ride and the type of horse you learn on, you will find various additional equipment may be included as part of your horse's tack. These will be intended to help you as a beginner rider and the horse as a carrier of a beginner rider. Such gadgets can be simple or more complicated. Among the most basic you will come across is an old stirrup leather fastened around the horse's neck. The idea with this is that it gives you something to grab hold of if you feel unbalanced at any point and it saves the horse's mouth, which would otherwise bear the brunt of your attempts to balance yourself on the reins. In some schools, side reins or draw reins are used to produce the correct

Tip

+ Secure and correctly fastened equipment does not cause the horse any physical or psychological damage, in fact, it does just the opposite – it prevents it. It makes no sense for the horse to constantly suffer at the hands of inexperienced riders who would be very unhappy if they knew the discomfort they were inadvertently causing.

comfort, cause all sorts of distress to their horse simply because they dislike asking for help in getting the best from him. I hate to describe the sort of behaviour you might see but it includes yanking the horse at the front, and constantly attacking him with spurs behind. This type of riding is completely ineffectual – it is agonizing for the horse and will eventually break his spirit. Then the rider blames the horse for its poor performance, gets rid of it, buys another and the whole cycle begins again.

I hope that you have chosen a riding school that won't tolerate this sort of riding and that you will quickly recognize a rider like this.

If any sort of additional equipment is fitted to your school horse, just calmly ask why, how it works, how to fit it, and so on. It's all part of the learning process.

shape in the horse so that you only have to worry about what you are doing, which is to learn how to sit in balance on the horse.

When you are doing exercises at a walk you will have no need of any of these items, because the gentle movement allows you to keep co-ordinated while sitting and you might even be able to try some steering. At a trot, however, you might find that your capabilities are overloaded and you are grateful for the extra help. Unfortunately, there are plenty of riders who, from lack of skill or though ignorance or just for their own

Left: Stephanie's riding skills are backed up by the use of loosely fitted side reins.

Above: Thank you for not throwing me off, Aztec's stand-in!

Sitting exercises in the saddle

The exercises below are designed to develop your sensitivity.

They should prepare you for your first session on the lunge, when you'll be sitting in the saddle, almost like a real rider.

Feng Shui for the backside

It's now time to get ready for sitting in the saddle. So that you can feel at home, we'll start with a slightly less than comfortable position. Do a half 'Mill' on the saddle, so that you're sitting backwards, looking over the horse's croup. Your backside will soon tell you something is wrong, because the saddle is designed for sitting forwards. Don't worry, all you do is sit here for a few minutes, then you can turn round the right way. When you turn around you will have an instant comfort reaction. What a wonderful saddle. This exercise is partly a psychological trick so that you'll love your saddle, rather than crying for your lovely saddle pad and girth. For further work on horseback, and to look after the horse's back, the saddle is indispensable.

Before you mounted, you will have adjusted the length of the stirrups. Put your feet back into them and make yourself comfortable, then we'll take the horse into a walk. You can choose whether to do this on the lunge or with someone leading you. You have plenty of time now to get used to the feeling of sitting in the saddle, and you should practise over and over slipping your feet out of the stirrups and getting them back in as quickly as

you can. It is important to practise this so that it works in reality, for example, if your foot comes out of a stirrup the first time you try trotting. If you've practised, you'll be able to fish successfully for the stirrup with your foot. If you don't succeed in getting your foot back in at once, you can always halt the horse by pressing both knees against the saddle, and then help yourself out with a hand to replace your stirrup.

But now you're calmly on your way, and you have all the time in the world to practise.

This is where it is important to have the right footwear. Well-designed riding boots make slipping your foot in and out of the stirrup easy and keeping it there easy too. You've come all this way, learnt so much, and you haven't come to any harm. Up next is a lunge session. Now you're off. Look forward to it!

The seat

'Take your seats, please!' Easily said, but carrying out this instruction is one of the greatest challenges riding has to offer. Many factors have a role to play in attaining an ideal seat on horseback.

Many riding instructors' directions are restricted to 'Head up, shoulders back, back straight, lower leg back, heels down!' and the result is often a totally cramped posture. This is because as a beginner rider you will be exclusively focused on her separate body parts and your attempts to co-ordinate them. But the whole thing also has to take place in combination with the unfamiliar motion of the horse's body. A loose, supple seat, with free muscles and the right amount of physical tension, is not achievable in such circumstances. It's a great pity that so many instructors are like a dog with a bone in their attachment to this ideal image of a seat, because they completely ignore the possibility that a student might come to them with good basic posture, which they could then gradually refine and improve.

There is no question that a correct, relaxed seat is vital for the production of the dynamic balance with which a rider can influence the horse by the subtlest of signals. But the methods of attaining this goal must be considered.

The value of a deep, balanced seat

Although there are many different riding styles in the world, a clear, common goal among them is to have a balanced seat, which means to have even weight distribution in the rider and, as far as possible, a matching of the centres of gravity of horse and rider. This is the only way that both horse and rider can progress in their skills and stay fit and healthy in the long run.

Here are some of the factors working against the ideal seat from the outset. A badly trained or inadequately trained horse will not move correctly and so will not enable the rider to sit loosely and evenly. An ill-fitting saddle that causes the horse pain will make it restricted in its movements. Even if it doesn't hurt, a saddle that fits poorly can affect the horse's movements through its effect on the rider's body. For instance, if the rider is not sitting over the centre of gravity, but too far back

Take heart – not all riding is this uncomfortable.

towards the loins, this will influence the horse's ability to walk or trot smoothly and freely. The rider, too, has to contend with innate or habitual bad posture. It is difficult to follow the directions of the instructor if you are firstly a beginner, and secondly have a slight curvature of the spine brought about by wear and tear. How many horses are out there that can walk straight with a swinging back under a perfectly fitting saddle? How many riders are out there with absolutely no physical problems, who are able to sit perfectly correctly at the centre of gravity, as if poured into the saddle? How often do you think these ideal conditions arise together?

That's right. Very few and very seldom.

To a beginner, any rider of many years' experience can look like a miracle on horseback. Sadly, though, even with advanced riders, there can be tricks lurking behind an ideal façade. For example, to compensate for an unbalanced seat they might hold tightly on the reins,

squeezing with their thighs and hollowing the small of their back to hide a heavy seat. So, spare yourself the agony of going down that road.

If you read this book carefully you will be guided towards the ideal seat, but step by step, and without destroying your own natural posture. Through the exercises used here, you can work on bringing yourself into balance, and on refining and perfecting your natural seat so that it's safe and suited to what we know of the movement patterns of the horse.

Even the exercises you have already done, which involve turning around on a still horse, help with the development of a good seat. Because you only happily sit down where you feel comfortable, don't you? The ones where you sit on a bare back and feel the horse's

Info

+ A healthy balance between tension and relaxation is a goal worth striving for, and will improve the subtlety of your sensitivity beyond belief.

muscles moving beneath you help because a sure feel for the horse's movement patterns is a basic requirement for a good sense of balance. These sensory exercises also benefit your sense of your own weight distribution.

The ideal seat

– You sit, with the muscles of your seat quite loose, evenly under both seat bones.
– Your knees lie with the flat inner side against the saddle. The lower legs hang slightly backwards against the horse's ribs.
– You are keeping close contact with the horse through the flat inside of your calves.
– The stirrups are beneath the balls of your feet, and your weight is as even as possible on each. Your toes are pointing slightly away from the horse. Your ankles are free to let your weight pass down across your heels.
– Your upper body is upright, your chest is open and your shoulders are going gently back, not being hunched upwards.

This is not perfection, but Stephanie's doing her best and she will get better.

- You are carrying your head freely and upright.
- Your arms hang easily by the sides of your upper body. At the elbow, they bend with your forearms held loosely across your body.
- You carry your hands closed and vertical, thumbs lying on the reins.
- Seen from the side, your shoulders, your hips and your heels should be in line vertically.

Every beginner rider comes with some elements of this sitting plan already in place. These elements must be built up and developed, which is the exact opposite to cramping up. Patience, lots of practice and refined work are now required, of you, of your instructor and – at least as far as patience is concerned – your school horse.

The oft-repeated phrase 'You only learn riding by riding!' is still one of the most honest sayings in the whole riding world.

Get yourself showered with gifts, for Christmas, Easter, Whitsun, May Day, your birthday, everybody else's birthday, Valentine's Day, bank holidays and all the days in between. And let the gifts be... riding lessons!

Be careful if you wear rings. They can catch on fastenings or chafe your fingers. It's better to leave jewellery at the stable.

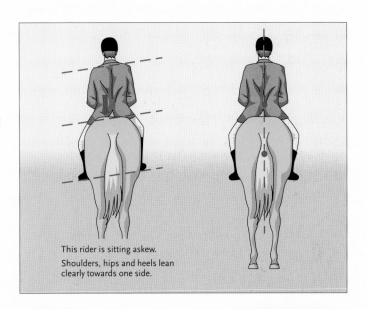

This rider is sitting askew. Shoulders, hips and heels lean clearly towards one side.

A variant: the light seat

For jumping or riding cross-country, a light seat is preferred. You're going to learn this now because it gives you another experience of how to balance and it's a good way to learn how to absorb the horse's movement at the trot.

Shorten your stirrups by two or three holes, to ease your balance in the stirrups. Sit calmly in the saddle and lithely following the horse's movements. Still seem too difficult for you? Let's try. Trot on. Don't be afraid. It's no different from when you were holding the surcingle grip, and your instructor can always help you if you need it.

Dry runs

+ To maintain an upright position with shoulders going back, try this:

+ While taking a pleasant walk with your dog or some other partner of your choice, fold your hands behind your back. This tightens your upper body, and you will become more upright at once.

+ This position is often called the teacher's walk, and there is a certain truth in this. It lends an aura of concentration and interest, and also a certain authority, by raising up the whole person. Try it out for its effects, and also to get your body used to this posture.

Patient correction of the seat in every situation is something you can expect of a good instructor.

Also, if you need to, you can rest your hands to the left and right of the mane on the horse's neck to help your balance or use a neckstrap for support if one is provided. With the measured help of both your legs, and again of your voice, give the signal to trot on. Now, practise the light seat. Your backside remains on the saddle, but not deeply in it. Your upper body bends forward a little, so that it is now supported more through the thighs and knees on the horse's sides. Keep the lower legs where they were, and don't let them slide backwards.

This sitting position will make your first trot easier,

The light seat

+ helps with the training of young horses whose back musculature is not yet fully developed.

+ is best for cross-country riding, to protect the horse's back when going over uneven ground, and to allow quicker reactions.

+ is often used in the training of jumping horses, when a quick change of sitting position is needed.

because your weight, which you are not yet able to swing up and down smoothly using your hips in the rising trot, can be softly absorbed by the give in your hips, knees and ankles.

One more step: the jumping seat

Now lift your bottom a little way out of the saddle and push it back slightly. Lean your upper body forward a little, and use your hands to really support yourself on the horse's neck. Be careful that your shoulders, elbows and wrists don't become stiff, but stay free. Push your feet a little more into the stirrups, so that it's easier for you to balance on them. Make sure there is still some give in your knee and hip joints. Your lower legs rest quietly on the horse's ribs, without sliding backwards. Don't try to sustain this seat for ten circuits at a time. Have walking breaks every so often so that you can recover. But then go on, because you need to practise to

achieve control over your body. It doesn't come all that easily.

If you find this hard work, remember that a light seat is also needed for having lovely long canters in the country. A hot shower when you've finished will relieve the worst of your muscular aches. Have a nice evening, and be proud of yourself.

Wonderful! Stephanie is balancing herself and even stretching out one hand to the side.

A little theory –
the aids

As a rider, you have various options for influencing your horse. The so-called 'aids' are the means of communication you can use from the saddle.

You can achieve influence over the horse by using:
– your weight and breathing
– leg position and pressure
– reins
– your voice.

All these aids, used in suitable combinations, make up the language you use to tell your horse what you want from him. It takes years of practice to make these communication skills perfect, so that they are invisible to onlookers. But don't be put off, we all have to start somewhere.

Dry run

+ Take someone by the shoulders, and get this person to lean to the side unexpectedly. Whoops! You'll need a few steps to restore your balance.

Weight distribution and breathing

It's easy for you as a beginner to understand weight distribution, even in practice. The horse follows a physical law, walking under your centre of gravity in order to remain in balance himself. The **weight aids** are divided into symmetrical pressure, one-sided pressure and pressure relief, and they are used to steer the horse and control his speed.

Let's look at steering first

To ride a turn, you direct your weight precisely on to one seat bone – the one in whose direction you want to ride. For example, if you want to turn left, increase the pressure on your left-hand seat bone, so giving the horse the first impulse to follow your turn. The horse will always make an effort to follow your weight, in order to restore his own balance. In this instant, tip your left (inside) hip forwards and your right (outside) hip backwards. It's best if you also look in the direction you want to ride in as you turn, because then your right shoulder (the outside shoulder in this case) will also automatically turn forwards.

During this weight shift, do not buckle to the left in your left hip. This would reverse the conditions, making the right seat bone work directionally on the horse (see the illustration opposite for an example of a buckled right hip). By the way, have you noticed what happens to your inside knee when you alter the balance of your seatbones? It drops.

Stephanie is turning nicely in the direction of movement.

Throughout the whole turn, you must keep your upper body upright. As soon as you want to ride straight ahead again, straighten your pelvis and your shoulders once more. Sensitive, well-trained horses can be steered this way and that across the riding arena using these weight aids alone, even without a bridle.

Symmetrical weight aids allow you to influence the horse's speed. Raising your upper body, combined with tensing your seat muscles, either requires your horse to push harder with its hindlegs, or has a slowing effect. It probably sounds rather confusing that the same thing can achieve two completely different results. This is where the combination of weight, leg and rein aids plays its part, as does the horse's fitness. If the horse willingly follows the onward-driving weight and leg aids, and at the same time accepts the restraining rein aid, in other words stretches at the poll, he has achieved a high level of fitness and training. This co-ordination from back to front, and the consequent curve in his body, allows the horse to be ridden a bit like a concertina. This is an instrument that only sounds good at a certain level of tension. If you overstretch it, you break it, and if you squeeze it together, it won't make any sound.

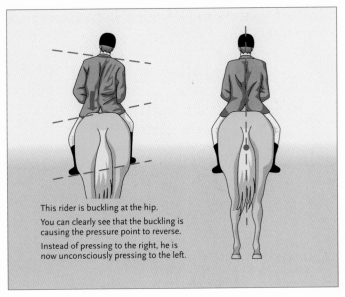

This rider is buckling at the hip.

You can clearly see that the buckling is causing the pressure point to reverse.

Instead of pressing to the right, he is now unconsciously pressing to the left.

Tip

+ **Rule of thumb for all turns:**

  Outside shoulder and inside hip go forward.

Pressure relief aids are used with quite young horses, or when walking backwards. Here, you shift your weight more on to your legs, without, however, taking your seat out of the saddle.

Your breathing can always work to support the weight aids. For example, when you breathe in clearly, your body becomes taut and lifts. When you consciously exhale, it relaxes and tends to fall. This can be enough to halt a sensitive horse, even from quicker paces. You can use regular breathing to regulate the rhythm, or speed of each pace, and you can also have a calming effect in stressful situations by continuing to breathe evenly and calmly.

Leg position and pressure

Your lower legs should stay lightly and quietly on the horse's body, just as they were in the seat exercises you learned earlier. Use leg aids for changes of direction and/or tempo. With the support of the other aids such as voice or weight, the legs are used to send a measured impulse – with the emphasis on 'measured' – so as to sustain the message that you are giving to the horse.

You should employ your leg aid only when something is required, and release it as soon as this has been achieved. Your leg can drive on or restrain. The *driving leg* gives its impulse near to the saddle girth. The *restraining leg* works about a hand's breadth further back on the ribcage. On winding paths, you will need one and then the other in combination. Riding in a clockwise circle, your right (inside) leg will be driving on the girth,

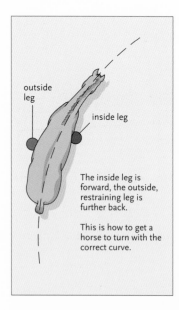

outside leg

inside leg

The inside leg is forward, the outside, restraining leg is further back.

This is how to get a horse to turn with the correct curve.

and your left (outside) leg restraining behind the girth. This restraining leg is only there as a support to ensure that the horse turns along its whole longitudinal axis, rather than just pushing out its hindquarters and turning more or less straight, without extending its muscles.

In more advanced exercises like leg yielding (asking the horse to walk

Mutual trust and good training are the basis of a team like this.

Info

+ Your leg always influences the hind leg of the horse on the same side.

sideways), you will also learn to use your leg to *drive the horse to the side*.

The degree of leg impulse, or leg pressure, should always start at the gentlest, finest extreme, and only be increased as necessary.

Below: Leg aids can only be given well if the stirrup is correctly positioned on the balls of the feet.
Right: This is where the driving leg must lie.

Rein aids

First, hold the reins with closed, but not clenched, fingers, and have the part that runs to the horse's mouth between the ring finger and little finger. Imagine that you have a tiny, delicate bird between your fingers, so that there is no chance of your hand balling into a fist. Your hands are upright, and the thumbs lie loosely open on the reins, at the same time also touching the index fingers, over which the rein end runs. You can now give appropriate rein aids through your loose wrist. These aids can work in opposition, in release, and in restraint.

The rein of *opposition* is mostly used when changing to a slower gait, when regulating tempo, when stopping or introducing certain exercises, also when directing to the side. The degree of pull you exert depends on the quality of the weight or leg aids you have already given. If they

were good, you only need the lightest touch on the horse's mouth. You must never just pull back.

You can imagine what torture a piece of iron can be in a horse's mouth if it's used without sensitivity. So please always choose the gentlest form of communication you can. Often a tiny pressure of your finger is enough to attract the horse's attention.

Here, too, as soon as you get the reaction you're looking for, replace the rein of opposition with a releasing rein aid. Depending on the situation, release can be used to get the horse to stretch out completely. The restraining rein has a similar purpose to the restraining leg. As soon as you give an aid to turn left and direct the horse's neck with your left (inside) rein, give a restraining or limiting rein aid with the right (outside) rein. *Restraining* just means keeping contact as far as you're concerned. But take care never to let your outside hand stiffen up. It also has to allow the desired position to come about. Follow the ripple of

movement as far as you wish, making sure that you have the horse on both reins. Don't let the outside rein hang loose.

Ensure that you keep the rein contact to the horse's mouth as soft and elastic as possible. Never use the reins for pulling or holding on, because that's not what they were designed for. No matter what you might see supposed professionals doing during your riding career, do not be misled into being rough with your horse. Well-known riders are not always good riders, and even good riders can make mistakes.

Voice

Your voice is an important part of your aid repertoire. Stupidly, it's often frowned upon to work with the horse on a verbal level. But it brings great benefits both to horse and rider. Please tell me what is so dreadful about a horse learning to stop at a softly whispered 'Whoa!' or cantering on at the word 'canter', without your having to use any other aid? Nothing! Of course it's sensible for the horse to know and react to all the other aids as well,

The fingers should be loosely closed, never clenched up.

otherwise this horse would have to bring along a dictionary of its vocabulary for other riders to use. But a broad training that also includes sensitivity to the voice has never harmed a horse.

It's also much easier, when necessary, to calm a horse that is aware of the voice, or to reinforce other orders. You can read up more about the use of the voice when thinking about measuring how much aid you need to give.

It will take you quite some time to become familiar with all these aids and to learn to use them appropriately for their various purposes. You need to be able to use them in all kinds of different combinations, so you have plenty on your plate.

But right now, it is a pleasure to see you marching, step by step, in the right direction. Just make sure you don't take a wrong turning – ask your horse for advice now and again, it understands you well.

Info

+ A well-trained horse will react to the mere transmission of a thought from his rider.

+ This is not an exaggeration, but sadly it is rare.

+ If you work hard enough you will achieve this wonderful connection with the horse. It will be worth all the effort, I can assure you.

What do you think, Molly, did I do it right?

Less is more!

Perhaps you're surprised by how little physical effort is needed to control and guide a horse. But that is the idea of all riding: minimizing the aids, achieving harmonious work with the subtlest communication.

There is a basic concept that applies to all aids. Always start with the minimal amount. If the horse doesn't do what you have asked, repeat your request – the aid – a

In groundwork...

... people often talk about applying and releasing pressure. Here's a simple example to explain this theme.

+ If you want a horse to move out of the way and you nudge it with your finger, you have applied pressure in the truest sense of the word.

+ As soon as the horse takes a step in the direction you want, stop nudging it, instantly.

+ The horse now makes this association: Nudging means that I have to move. OK, I'll do that. I must have got that right. Next time I'll do it when I see a finger stretched out towards me.

+ If you had continued nudging, the horse would have learned nothing. He would have become unsure, perhaps even quarrelsome, because he would not understand that he had already done what you asked.

little more vigorously. If that isn't enough, perhaps you could add another, different kind of aid. Once you get the desired reaction, stop your exhortations at once, and give the horse positive feedback. 'That's right, that was exactly what I wanted.'

There can never be an absolutely rigid schedule of procedures when you are working with a living creature, but there can and must be basic guidelines for you to learn and practise.

Be controlled – and use your voice

While riding, of course, you must have not only your body but also your voice under control. Outbreaks of verbal rage are quite inappropriate when working with a horse. The correct approach is to use precisely targeted words that are sharp and increasing in volume as a warning. This signals to the horse that your message is a serious one.

Always use bright, short, sharp sounds when using your voice for making demands and attracting attention. For a calming or restraining effect, choose long, rich vocal sounds.

When working on the lunge, make the order to step up a pace as 'walk on,' 'tarrott' or 'canter' with the stress on the second syllable. If you want to bring the gait back down, say calmingly 'waaaaaalk on' or 'teeeeeeerrott'. Stress the first syllable. Adding a rich 'whoa!' can reinforce the effect.

Precise use of the voice also involves free, even breathing. It won't do any good if your voice sticks and you can't get a word out because you aren't breathing properly. Learn to use both voice and breathing precisely. When you breathe in, notice how your whole body tenses up, and feel how you collapse as you

breathe out. Good aids to learning correct breathing are elements of self-hypnosis or Feldenkrais work (see page 70).

Fine-tuning – that is, the right measurement of all aids that we have at our disposal with the horse – can be practised. You just have to work at it. Just start a 'conversation' with any horse whenever you're at the stable. And if you're thinking 'I'll never learn that!' I would like to answer you in the words of Confucius. 'The way is the destination.'

....

Left: Don't be afraid, Molly, it's only a fish.
Below: A good many horses will perform works of art like the 'Spanish walk' on voice commands alone.

....

And so, on to the horse!

Lunge sessions in the
saddle

Now it's time for a few lunge sessions in the saddle. This is where you get to experience something that is pretty close to real riding.

During lunge lessons you learn to ask your horse to move forward and to stop if appropriate, too. You will learn how to use the reins with caution and you will also do a variety of seat exercises to prepare yourself for your first longer riding experiences. Your instructor will provide you with extra confidence by being at the end of the lunge rein.

Where's the accelerator?

To start into a walk, do this:
– Tilt your pelvis to press your hips forward, and at the same time use both legs on the girth to give the signal to go – as subtly as possible, of course. If you're cunning, you will also have secretly, quietly whispered 'walk on!'
– Don't forget to take off the handbrake. If you have a connection with the horse's mouth, gently open your fingers when asking the horse to walk on, so that he understands, 'Ah, forwards!'
– If you leave the gates closed ahead of you by not loosening the rein contact, your horse might think he is being asked to go backwards, because the aid combination of driving legs and holding hands is usually used to get a horse to go backwards.

So your horse is now walking. What do you do if he starts to dawdle and you want him to keep up a steady pace? You press his sides alternately with your legs. With each step he takes, you can feel that one leg has a stronger contact with the horse's ribs. At this moment, the horse is lifting a hind foot. If you identify this moment precisely, you can use your aids to encourage the horse to lift his feet more energetically and make a better step. This means the horse is almost creating the aid for himself through his movement. He will step

A final tightening of the girth and then you're off.

tep ^{by} Step

Practical test

1 Stretch your arms out sideways and start with some hip-turning exercises. Swing both arms around, reaching out as far as you can, first in one direction, then the other.

Always let your head go in the direction of the turn. Your seat stays in the saddle.

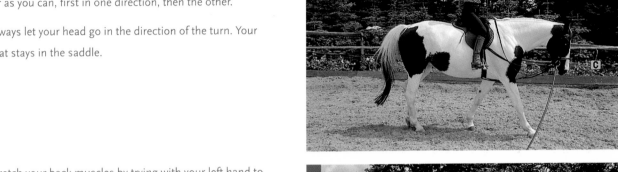

2 Stretch your back muscles by trying with your left hand to touch the tip of your right toe, and vice versa. This teaches you to keep your knee on the saddle and so keep your balance when you need to.

Never lower your head too far in this exercise, otherwise it will fall victim to the planet's gravitational force.

3 Now let's stretch your thigh muscles a bit. Take hold of the right ankle with your right hand and lift it as far as you can, without lifting your knee off the saddle panel.

Do the same exercise on the left side, and, if you dare, both at once. Repeat all these exercises a few times. Please don't forget to breathe freely and evenly during all exercises.

Info

+ In some schools you'll be taught to drive every pace, every step and every canter skip. This doesn't seem sensible to me, because it results in desensitization to the leg.

+ It makes much more sense to give a clear signal and, when this is correctly answered, to end it, until you want to do something new, or the horse stops doing as he has been asked – when he will need a reminder to continue.

more cleanly under his centre of gravity, and will begin to take more load on his hindquarters, moving it off his forequarters. This is a big step in the direction of keeping your horse in good health.

Remember though – little and often

Please don't use your leg all the time, and never without planning it out first. If the horse is back in the rhythm you want, let your leg rest against his ribcage. If the rhythm, or its expression, changes, drive on again. Basically, you should be aiming to develop a feel for each horse you ride. If you have enough capacity for sensation, you'll soon know how much aid it's best to give. Which brings me back to one aim of the whole business of riding, which is to minimize aids.

Now you've managed to walk on successfully. To get you looser, and to train your sense of balance, we're now going to do a few physical exercises.

So where are the brakes?

Lay the reins on the horse's neck, because you don't need them for the moment. Now you are going to ask your horse to stop. Finally, you can use the breathing skills that you've been practising for so long. Use your whole repertoire of aids for stopping. Always starting with the lightest aid possible.

As you were so good at using your voice for walking on, you can also try a soft 'halt!' or 'whoa!' As a beginner rider you should be familiar with all the possibilities. Ride on in walk. Try stopping, using your seat and breathing.

Sit more upright and a little heavier in the saddle and, at the same time, give a conscious, deep, long exhalation. Your lower legs stay calmly and evenly on the horse. Excellent, it's stopped. Ride on again and then stop again. Try to get the horse to do what you want. If you have slowed your breathing and relaxed your body in advance, it will react more subtly to you. Well done.

A knack for using the reins properly

Walk on again, and pick up the reins. Hold the reins between your ring and little fingers, and create a subtle, light contact with the horse's mouth. Make sure the reins are of equal length, and not twisted, your hands upright and resting over the horse's withers. As your horse walks, his head makes a nodding movement, which you will be able to feel through the reins. Make an effort to follow this nodding motion gently. Definitely don't let your hands stiffen up.

With the support of your seat and your breathing, you're now going to give your first rein aids. Decide on a spot where you want to stop. When you're nearly there, give out tiny impulses from your (uncramped) fingers through the reins to the horse's mouth. As you're in walk, a slow gait, these impulses might need only be the slightest feel on the reins in order to stop the horse. So try just squeezing the ring finger towards the palm of your hand. If this isn't enough, repeat it softly several times. Because your horse was already sensitized to stopping exercises without the reins, it should respond well to this gentle signal from the rein.

You can spare the horse's mouth by learning with a bitless bridle (see page 108), if your horse has been trained to use it. But your hands still need to learn to work subtly and precisely, and the key thing you need to practise is to sit independently of the reins – which means you don't use the reins for balance.

What you learn now about the use of your weight and the breathing aids will be helpful to you throughout your riding life.

A contented friend!

Better late...

than never

+ I rode for the first time when I was about 20 years old, on holiday in the Camargue. I'd dreamed about this moment since I was a child. After that holiday, I didn't ride again for a long time. When I was 40 I had another go, also on holiday, this time in Hungary, but it was terribly stressful.

+ When my daughter, Julia, started to ride, I often looked on longingly over the arena fence. When the riding school started up a course for adults, I applied and I have never regretted it. We work quietly in a small group, which is perfect. I love being with the horses without being afraid and I'm really enjoying the riding.

+ Meanwhile, all sorts of horsey books are piling up on my bedside table, because I want to know more and more about horses. I hope in the end that I'll be able to ride with my daughter but at the moment I'm happy just learning.

Margaret, 48

Rising trot – how easy can a
trot be?

'Easy? At last! Something effortless!' you're thinking? Far from it, although this time, it isn't muscular effort we're after, but a sense of rhythm.

As you've already gained some confidence through working at balancing at the trot using the light seat (see page 90), the rising trot will be a piece of cake. Keep your body loose and relaxed, and don't think too much in circles, but instead focus on the rhythm of movement. It really isn't that difficult to learn.
A proper rising trot spares the horse's back and allows beginner riders in particular to follow the horse's movements more easily. And, at the same time, you won't tire out as quickly.

Roland enjoying the rising trot.

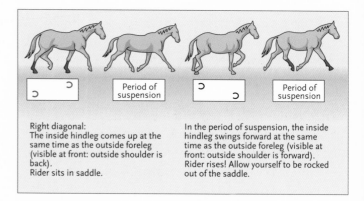

Right diagonal:
The inside hindleg comes up at the same time as the outside foreleg (visible at front: outside shoulder is back).
Rider sits in saddle.

In the period of suspension, the inside hindleg swings forward at the same time as the outside foreleg (visible at front: outside shoulder is forward).
Rider rises! Allow yourself to be rocked out of the saddle.

How it works

Supported by your knees and the stirrups, let the swinging rhythm of the horse gently raise you out of the saddle on every other trot step, and then sit back down for the next trot step. You must land softly in the saddle, otherwise you can forget that bit about 'sparing the horse's back'. You don't get extra marks in the rising trot for rising a long way. On the contrary, it should just be a gentle rocking movement. The movement of your particular horse will determine how much or little you're taken out of the saddle. It's important to sit back down with your seat pushed forward, and without hollowing your back. Catch your weight with your knees, and let them 'give' it down into your ankles.
To start with, it's often helpful if you count a rhythm aloud to yourself.
You already know that the trot is in double time: left diagonal leg pair, right diagonal leg pair, left pair, right pair, and so on.

If you kept this same rhythm going as you trotted around for an hour, you'd constantly be putting pressure on the horse's same hind leg. This is because you are always coming back into the saddle as he lifts a back foot from the ground. However, it is possible to sit when the other back foot lifts off the ground because the trot is a symmetrical pace. You do this by 'changing the diagonal', which ensures that your horse is bearing an even load. It's easy. As you're counting aloud, throw in an extra beat and stay sitting in the saddle during that beat. Like this: 'One – sit – change – one'. Stay seated for both 'sit' *and* 'change' and rise again for the next 'one', then resume counting as normal: 'One – sit, one – sit', and so on. You will have changed the diagonal.

Trotting in the school

During schooling work in the arena you should always rise out of the saddle on the hind leg that is to the inside. As you don't have eyes in the back of your head, and you might not quite have developed a complete sense of the pace sequence, you might think it will be difficult to know how to do this. But you've read the description of the basic pace thoroughly, so you do

T i p

+ At first, count along in the rising trot like this: 'one – sit, one – sit, one – sit'. Once you have the rhythm, concentrate at 'one' on rising from the saddle, and at 'sit' on sitting down again. Don't feel self-conscious about counting aloud, it really helps you keep the rhythm.

T i p

+ When you're riding for longer periods in open country later, you should always change the rhythm periodically so as to give the horse a balanced workout.

know which leg to watch to get the right rhythm for rising. Just to spell it out – when the inside hind leg is swinging forward (which you can't see, and might not be able to feel yet), simultaneously, the outside – diagonal – shoulder is going forward (which you can see easily). That is the moment at which you should be out of the saddle. As the inside hind foot strikes the ground, the outside shoulder comes back and the outside foreleg touches the ground too. That is the moment at which you should be sitting in the saddle. (See page 118 for a full explanation of inside and outside, but for the moment 'inside' is the side of the horse that is nearest the inside of the school and 'outside' is the side nearest to the outside of the school.) If you still have difficulty understanding when to rise and sit, look again at the diagrams of the trot sequence on page 104.

Well, that's enough for today. Come back to a walk, praise your horse – and thank your instructor – because they will have both been on tenterhooks during your first trot.
Once you've looked after your horse and he is in the stable or paddock enjoying a munch, go and swop stories with your fellow riders and see how they got on during their first rising trot.

Free
at last!

Now you are ready to ride without someone on the ground either next to the horse's head or at the end of a lunge line. The basic goal is still to use the subtlest possible aids to achieve harmonious communication with the horse. But, since beginners often have particular difficulties with the use of the reins, this will be an area of focus.

A little bit
about bits

As I've already said, one of the most direct ways that you communicate with a horse is through his mouth.

The mouth is a very sensitive part of the horse. With it he can tell whether he is eating grass or hay, leaves or an apple. If you put a small stone into a horse's feed bowl, along with the food, he will be able to tell it is there and avoid eating it through feeling it with his mouth and lips (he can't see it because his nose is in the way). It therefore follows that a bit is a very powerful tool in the right hands and a possible instrument of torture in the wrong ones.

Every beginner rider, and a good number of more experienced ones, should play at being the horse, and get an idea of how a bit works. No, don't worry, you don't need to gallop panting and groaning around the riding arena with a piece of metal between your teeth and a fellow rider on your back. It's enough for you, in the role of the horse, to take the bit in both hands. A

colleague now takes the reins and pulls gently on them. Try it in turns, to find out what movements you feel in your hands, coming through from the reins. You will be amazed at how clearly the slightest change can be felt.

Improving hand signals

Once I have introduced riders to this sensation I like to improve hand signals and the use of independent rein aids by using a bitless bridle. A horse that has learned to turn from the pressure of the headcollar on his face in the course of groundwork will respond well in a bitless bridle.

To turn right, take the reins out sideways to the right (do not pull them back!), and the horse will take his head to the right. He follows the pull of the right rein, and turns away from the pressure that he feels on the left-hand side of his nose. For you as a beginner rider, these first attempts in the riding arena are a wonderful opportunity to practise steering without fear of hurting his mouth.

You can now practise guiding your horse this way and that, through obstacles and the zigzag of poles you met in the leading exercises, by using the combination of weight, leg and voice aids you've learned.

It's very much a question of technique rather than muscles. For example, you should be able to stop the horse like you did when he was wearing a bitted bridle, just by squeezing on the reins.

What is a bitless bridle?

+ The bitless bridle, or hackamore, is like a normal bridle but the reins are attached to the noseband via rings which may be on the noseband itself or at the end of long shanks.

A correctly fitted bitless bridle.

Sensitive use of the snaffle

Once you have had some practise with a bitless bridle you will probably feel more confident when riding with a simple snaffle bridle again. One of the most important things to remember as a beginner rider is to keep your hands and wrists soft and to go with the movement of the horse's neck and mouth. Don't worry, he's not planning on shooting off

Improving your
dexterity

+ You can practise your dexterity while grooming your horse. Use the brushes equally in both hands.

+ Become a virtuoso of the currycomb. Make bigger, stronger circles across the wide expanses of broad muscles, and smaller, more delicate ones across bonier areas.

+ Be very aware of the transitions from strong to delicate and make them fluent. Your horse will carry you through thick and thin after such a massage! You'll learn to keep your hand movements flowing, and that is important in the sensitive use of the rein-to-mouth connection.

Tip on how
to brake

+ If you want to slow your horse from an unintentional acceleration into a faster pace, turn his head and neck to the side by means of the clear use (but not pulling back!) of only one rein.

+ It's a waste of time, when a horse runs off in panic, to pull directly back on the bit or the bitless bridle. The animal's power is greater by far than the little pull you're able to exert.

anywhere. As you get more used to his natural movements you will gain confidence, but until then concentrate on using the minimum amount of rein aids. Don't, however, get hung up on not touching the horse's mouth at all. A horse is trained to 'take a contact' and most of them like to feel this link between the rider and themselves. They don't want you to slop along with flapping reins – it makes them feel insecure! Your instructor will tell you when you are getting it right and give you plenty of exercises and visual images to help. As your seat improves so will your rein aids. It just takes a little bit of time.

Fun ways to learn
new skills

It's easier to learn if you have a clear aim in mind. This applies to beginner riders just as much as it does to young horses, because with a clear aim, you understand much more quickly what is going on, and what is required of you.

To come to the point. It's much easier for beginners to learn how to ride a turn or circle correctly if they can ride around a visible obstacle. To achieve a similar circle in an empty, brushed riding arena requires much more effort. And the advantage of using an obstacle is that you can concentrate more on what you are doing than what your circle looks like – an egg?

The obstacle course

Barrels, hats and poles – you can use anything to ride around and they will all improve your riding skills. How is this so?
– Riding through a barrel slalom is wonderful training for your weight distribution, the positioning of your legs and your rein aids. It will also train the speed of your reactions, because even if you're only going at a walk, you have to react instantly to each barrel by manoeuvring your horse, as well as changing your seat.
– Riding through a corridor of poles teaches you to sit consciously straight, with an even distribution of weight between your two seat bones, and with both legs and reins steering absolutely straight. If you sit crookedly, you'll find yourself all over the place.
– Riding through a zigzag of poles gives you and your horse the first chance to practise sharp turns together.
– Riding through such a maze of poles on the ground is an excellent preparation for riding in open country where you might come across all sorts of obstacles in

This student has overdone the lean to the side. Just let more weight go on to the relevant seat bone.

Below: Stephanie practises the light seat while Flicka negotiates a collection of poles.
Bottom: Roland does a wonderful turn.

your path. At the same time it gives you another chance to practise your light seat.

It's supposed to be fun

While doing this kind of work, there should be a fun, relaxed atmosphere in the arena. You're learning to move on and with your horse in a playful way, and while you are concentrating on getting it right, you will also find that you forget your nerves. Your instructor will give you different challenges each time you ride through the obstacles such as try steering through using your weight and legs alone. However, don't let the fact that it's fun compromise the professional quality of your execution! The one thing does not exclude the other. If you like doing something, chances are also that you'll be more creative and aware when doing it. So, now go on to a long rein, ease off for a while and watch the others. You're doing well now, and the first group riding lesson is not far away. The way things are looking, you'll manage it with ease.

A co-operative partner

+ You know you benefit from this sort of work, but groundwork, walks, rides out, small jumps and general conditioning also train the horse to achieve ever higher levels of skill.

+ This work stimulates his thought processes, making him more and more sensitive and co-operative.

Meanwhile... riding out on a
lead rein

By the time you've got to this point, you might be thinking, 'I'll never be able to ride out of the school.'

However, even though you've some way to go before you're confident and competent enough to ride out on your own, there is nothing to stop you having a trip out while being led by your instructor.

Relax, you can do it

If your instructor suggests an outing, it will be because you're ready to give it a go. You've already learnt quite a bit about what goes on in open country from your walking exercises. The leading-rein rides will improve on this knowledge, and bring you yet another step closer to your goal of riding as an individual.

The reason why your first forays into the country are on a lead rein is for your own safety. This way you can continue to practise the effects of the various aids and experience your horse's behaviour in open country, and yet you won't be out of your depth.

In this situation, you and your horse are protected by your instructor who will ride beside you, which will increase your confidence, too. As your instructor and both horses have had plenty of experience, you are in good hands, and can just relax and enjoy yourself.

Don't daydream

It is normal practice for a horse that is being led to be on the inside of your instructor, away from other road users. This protects you and your horse, especially when traffic passes. This is also one way young, as yet unridden, horses are introduced to roads. But be careful. This is no excuse to daydream. Since your

Secured like this, riding out holds no fears.

instructor will occasionally have to make room for a passing vehicle, you might find yourself having to duck quickly under a branch or avoid some other obstacle. Enjoy it. It adds a bit of spice to the training session, and you'll learn to love your riding hat. It is also a good introduction to the sorts of hazards you will come across when you ride out on your own later on.

To duck under a branch, lie forwards, to the side of the horse's neck – as you've often practised before in your exercises. Don't come back up until you're absolutely sure that there are no twigs waiting to lash your face. Here's something else to practise. The horse you're riding should have his head around the level of the other horse's shoulder. It mustn't be forward of this point, and you as a rider must use your knowledge of the aids to work to maintain this position.

From your earlier leading work, you already know that this position puts your horse in the less dominant rank. So you are making it quite clear here that he must listen to rules from above – you in other words. This should also prevent him from starting an enthusiastic race with his colleague.

Riding in the country is no reason to abandon the regular, even rhythm that your practise in the school, or for letting the horse set his own pace. In other words, your horse must react to your weight, leg, rein and voice aids, just as if he were in the arena. In fact, if anything, even more precisely, because the situation might demand it. You can relax the rules a little once you're a better rider. Then you can spend some time idling on a long rein, or try a nice gallop to bring a shine to your eyes. For a gallop, you do have to be able to ride well, and know how to control your horse in every situation. For now, nice and safe next to your comforting instructor, you can gently practise your rising trot over longer distances. You'll see how wonderful it is

Flicka is on the lead rein so she is a little way behind Molly. Roland is free to practise the riding aids he's learned.

to trot for a longer period of time and mostly going straight, instead of turning at each school corner. Being able to trot for long periods of time will really help you find that harmonious rhythm. Don't forget to change the diagonal every now and then to work the horse equally on both sides.

Your instructor will be happy to answer any questions you might have about your horse or your riding technique. Soon you'll begin to feel what it is like to communicate with your horse on an ever more subtle level.

Your instructor summons you out of your dreams. Should we try a little canter? Oh, yes!

More preparations for
open country

When you've had a few trips out on the end of a lead rein, your next big experience will be going it alone – without the instructor 'safety net'.

Initially, you'll most likely do this in a field or other fairly enclosed space that is near the school. Your horse won't have any opportunity to take you on a trip of his own devising. Hopefully, this practice field will contain a few riding challenges for you to get your teeth into. You might find a bank, a ditch, some fallen branches or logs and various other obstacles dotted around. Don't panic.

This is not the Horse of the Year Show. You aren't going to be jumping over these obstacles, just learning how to deal with them.

Let's start with the bank. There's a huge difference between riding along on the flat and confronting a steep slope falling away at the edge of an embankment. And, you need to know what to do. This is why it is important to do this sort of practice in a safe place and in peace and quiet. Then, when you're riding out, the whole group won't have to turn round because you're scared of an embankment, or because you and the horse might come to harm because you don't know what to do.

balancing yourself at the same time with your hands on his neck. Be careful that you allow the horse enough freedom in the reins, because he will use his neck like a balancing pole. When riding downhill, you must also make sure that your horse goes down straight, so as not to lose his balance. This, too, you must achieve with the precise use of your leg and rein aids.

Now, if you are pleased with your attempts up and downhill, try the logs, which should be low enough to step over. In this situation it's best to leave your horse to sort himself out. He is much better at arranging his four legs without your interference. Either sit on him with a light seat, or dismount altogether. Let him get over them in peace on a long rein.

This is not just a short cut for beginners, it applies to advanced riders too. Use this technique for rough ground, as well. It is hard to do when you are going along a rocky path or beside a sharp drop, but you must allow the horse to pick his own way; he knows what he's doing, and he doesn't want to fall either.

With banks, logs and ditches, do bear in mind that your horse could get carried away with all the excitement. He might decide to trot down the slope for a bit of fun or leap over the log or ditch – it's easy. So be ready to sit down with a firmer seat and pull him up if necessary or to go with him should he leap, rather than getting left behind.

Left and above: Roland making his riding uphill and downhill debut. A very good effort.

Now all those aches and pains you got from practising the light seat are about to pay off. Lighten your seat – let your weight go into the stirrups, allowing give in your ankles.

When riding uphill or downhill, lean your upper body forward in relation to how steep the slope is, to relieve the pressure on the horse's back. The horse needs to be given this freedom in his back, because he needs to carry the weight of both of you, safely balanced, up or down the slope.

You must never try to keep your own balance by clenching your legs. This disturbs your horse's sense of balance and is giving him the wrong aids, too. It could result in a fall. Let the reins rest easy in both hands,

Tip

+ If you love horses, you must also love nature. Please always obey the Country Code when you go riding in open country.

be ridden in a particular way, and learning to time everything just right – takes much more time than there is in a couple of lessons on the lunge.

You will find the same applies throughout your riding career. All the new skills you learn will take time to become intuitive and second nature. And you will learn new things while you are still absorbing old ones. The same applies to training a horse. But, the more patient you are, the sooner you will see positive results.

You've come a long way in a short time and you're a pleasure to watch. Not because it's funny, but because you've really learned something. And it's so nice that after every practice session you take care of your horse. Be honest, without this interaction, something important would be missing, wouldn't it?

This is exactly why we practise these situations in the safety of a field. If he does jump, you'll have had the first little hop of your riding career, and you can feel proud of that afterwards. If you feel that your horse is going to jump, try to release the reins forward, so that he doesn't receive a painful jolt in his mouth.

You will now be able to vary your seat whenever you like. You've already learned in the riding arena to change from the light seat to the jumping seat, or back into the normal seat when it's time for a nice walk.

Now, if not before, you'll understand why you have learned and been taught in little steps. Learning to ride – developing the use of aids and refining your control for all sorts of situations, learning why the horse must

Above: Stephanie is balanced, and is not disturbing Flicka as she rides over the fallen tree trunk.
Right: Horse and rider have their minds on the job.

Finishing line in sight

You have now reached an important stage. Your thorough, slowly constructed foundation of work has brought you to the point where you can take part in 'normal' riding lessons without fear.

Your solid basic knowledge means that you are capable of reacting correctly to any given situation. Your

knowledge of a horse's anatomy, and the need for you to ride properly to ensure your horse's comfort, are developing apace.

Meanwhile, you no longer fear losing control of the horse, because you have some experience of the worst that could happen, and also of how to prevent it. Now and again, the thought has crossed your mind – admit it – that you might be able to manage a nice gallop. But you've also learned that false pride can only harm you and your horse. Think about it. You didn't learn your job overnight. You have a long period of training behind you, and you have that to thank for how good you are now. So give your hobby the chance of continuing to develop slowly but surely. If you do that, you'll never be bored or fed up, because there are always new challenges to seek.

Digression: inside and outside

When you're riding or watching other riders, you'll hear the instructor giving directions using the words 'inside' and 'outside' in relation to legs or reins or almost anything. But you may find that many of your riding colleagues, even those with several more years' experience than you, are unable to define exactly what 'inside' and 'outside' mean.

Learn it right from the start, and not just by the definition that 'inside' means where the riding

Kirsten is looking forward to her riding lesson.

Quietly discussing which order to ride in.

instructor is standing, and 'outside' is the fence. That is a good definition and it is usually sufficient, but not always. Here is a better rule of thumb. 'Inside' is always the concave, or hollow, side of the horse's neck. 'Outside' is always the convex, or lengthened, side of the horse. This means that when you are asked to do an exercise that bends the horse towards the fence, you still know where the inside is! The inside is always the horse's hollow side.

An instructor can easily show beginners this in the course of their exercises. Let's take the simple exercise of walking in a snaking line – called a shallow loop by those in the know (see diagram). You're riding anticlockwise – on the left rein – so the fence is to the right, and, up to now, it is the outside. But in order to steer the curving loop into the centre of the arena, you

have to change your horse's direction. Now, he is walking to the left, but is pointing to the right. The shortened, hollow side is thus towards the fence. So, in this case, for as long as this hollowing continues, the fence is the inside. A good instructor might at this point communicate a rein correction to a student, using the terms 'left' and 'right', so as not to be totally confusing. But at the end of the exercise, they should take time to explain what has happened to the inside and outside in this situation.

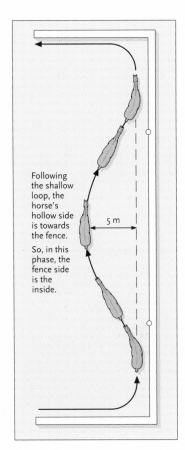

Following the shallow loop, the horse's hollow side is towards the fence.

5 m

So, in this phase, the fence side is the inside.

Your first 'normal' group lesson

The lesson you have today will be just as calm as all the lessons you've had up to now. An experienced rider will be at the head of the group, to make it easier for you to sustain a constant tempo. You'll do some circuits at a trot, but cantering will have to wait a little longer until you are all sure of each other. However, you should still be having the odd lead-rein ride, where you can enjoy a canter, or you might be learning more cantering skills on the lunge.

A dream come true.

Even if you are doing well and feel quite confident on your horse in a normal riding situation, fitting in occasional work on your seat on the lunge will do no harm. Apart from anything else, all these sorts of exercises are great fun.

Remember your instructor

It's so inspiring for an instructor to watch a protégé grow from being an interested, but still fearful beginner into a real horseman or horsewoman, conscious of their great responsibility to their equine partner. If both student and horse are enjoying their work, and the results are evident, then all the effort, patience and wear and tear on the nervous system have paid off. Don't forget to thank your instructor. She has made you the rider you are.

A final word – always remember that your partner is a living being and that he can't easily stick up for himself. Your route to being a rider may take you much further than you originally intended and along the way it won't just make you a good rider, but also a rider who every horse wants as a friend. And you can be proud of that, because horses don't pretend!

It should be fun!

+ Many riding instructors still seem to think that 'not screaming all the time is praise enough'. Don't you believe it. Like other sports – skiing, swimming, windsurfing, tennis – riding is fun. You do it for fun. You don't go along to be shouted at or reduced to tears. If your instructor sounds like a foghorn, get another.

My
wish
for the
future

Riding is not only about technical skill and physical sensitivity. Countless factors are involved in establishing a partnership with a horse.

There are only so many pages in this book, and I can't tell you *everything* about this subject here. However, if I have succeeded in giving at least some of you a good start, and encouraged you to think in the right way, so that you are well into the start of a harmonious life with horses, I'm grateful.

Being with a horse can enrich our lives beyond measure. We develop in every way through being able to communicate with a creature from another species. Horses can truly become our friends, and they can also expand our own circle of friends. This great gift is more than enough in return for our being conscious of our responsibility towards these animals.

Think of the moments of happiness that you have already experienced on horseback, and give horses the kind of treatment and life that their nature requires, so that they can live happily by our side.

Remark

+ Please never value your own sporting pride above the well-being of the horse. Apart from anything else, it won't do you any good!

Quo vadis, rider?

Where will your bridle path take you? Will you be a competitive rider, or a leisure rider? Actually, this is an unnecessary question, because the boundaries between these categories are dissolving. Just as well, because all types of riders can learn from each other.

So, what is the difference? Actually, there is less difference than you might believe. Competitive riders are not, as many leisure riders think, all ruthless, arrogant egoists, exploiting their horses and obsessed with playing to the gallery. On the other hand, neither are leisure riders all ignoramuses pootling about on sloppy horses. More and more competitive riders are beginning to realize the benefits of treating their horses as creatures not just performers. They

are finding that considering the needs of their horses and changing the way they keep them and ride them has a positive effect on how well the horses do in the show ring or across country. Care and kindness is always repaid by these generous animals. And, among leisure riders, there are more and more who are interested in keeping their horses fit and in good condition and who are good and keen classical riders who would no more dream of slopping about on their horse than they would think of leaving it hungry in the stable all day.

There's no reason why a horse that is treated properly and ridden well should not take part in competitions and look forward to winning a ribbon. Nor is there any legitimate objection to spending half an hour of an evening taking a leisure hack for a travers across the riding arena.

Use your leisure time for a sporting gallop or whatever you'd most like to do. Whatever you choose, do it so that everyone enjoys it. Even onlookers.

Acknowledgments

Thanks to all the two- and four-legged friends who took part in the photoshoots with such enthusiasm, and also to those who were kind enough to contribute their professional expertise. Many thanks to everyone at BLV who helped me in the creation of this book and gave their friendship and patience, especially my editor, Christa Klus-Neufanger, who helped to order my thoughts with great professionalism and consideration.

My most heartfelt thanks go to all the horses that have taught me so much through my life, despite not speaking my language.

Thanks, too, for the professional contributions from:
Eva-Maria Chiumento – B riding instructor, animal psychologist, neuro-linguistic programming practitioner
Sabine Nakelski – farrier, prospective hoof technician, Hoof and Claw Care Association, GdHK
Eva Rehm – physiotherapist
Kalle Rehm – equine osteopath (DIPO) and physiotherapist
Gabi Schreiber – educator, qualified riding instructor, Swiss Therapeutic Riding Association

Bibliography
and Further Reading

Kerstin Diacont, *Bodenarbeit mit Pferden (Groundwork with Horses)*, BLV

Monika Krämer, *Pferde erfolgreich motivieren (Successful Motivation of Horses)*, Kosmos

Monika Krämer, Jochen Schumacher, *Reiten lernen mit allen Sinnen (Learning to Ride With all the Senses)*, Kosmos

Heike Lebherz, *Sichtweisen – Positive Gedanken zu Mensch und Pferd (Ways of Seeing – Positive Thinking for Humans and Horses)*, FN-Verlag

Marie-Luise v.d. Sode, *Reiten nach M. Feldenkrais (Riding According to M. Feldenkrais)*, Cadmos

Michael Strick, *Denk-Sport-Reiten (Thinking Competitive Riding)*, FN-Verlag

Sally Swift, *Centered Riding*, St. Martin's/Marek, A Trafalgar Square Farm Book

Mary Wanless, *For the Good of the Horse*, Kenilworth Press

Useful Addresses

German Curatorium for Therapeutic Riding
Freiherr-von-Langen-Str. 13, 48231 Warendorf, Germany
Tel.: (+49) 25 81/6362-0; e-mail: dkthr@fn-dokr.de

British Horse Society
Stoneleigh Deer Park, Kenilworth, Warwickshire CV8 2XZ, England
Tel.: 08701 202 244; Fax: 01926 707 800, www.bhs.org.uk

Association of British Riding Schools
Queen's Chambers, 38–40 Queen Street, Penzance,
Cornwall TR18 4BH, England. Tel.: 01736 753045/369440

The American Horse Council
1616 H Street NW 7th Floor, Washington DC 20006, USA
Tel.: 00 1 202 296 4031; Fax. 00 1 202 296 1970;
www.horsecouncil.org/ahc.html

United States Pony Clubs Inc
4041 Iron Works Parkway, Lexington, Kentucky KY 40511-8462, USA
Tel.: 00 1 859 254 7669; Fax: 00 1 859 233 4652; www.ponyclub.org

Index